PRAI
WASTED BREATH

Not A Wasted Breath is a moving story of one courageous and remarkable child/man's life with cystic fibrosis. Todd gained enormous support from family, friends, and his community. I was privileged to be his doctor for eight years.

—H. David Wilson, MD, Professor of Pediatrics
Dean, University of Kansas School of Medicine, Wichita

Not a Wasted Breath is heart wrenching as Todd and his mom share a unique journey of anticipation, discouragement, sadness, joy, courage, compassion and most importantly faith, hope, and love ... I shed tears of laughter with Todd and tears of agony and loss with Mom.

—Sandy Hickey [donor mom]
Director Family Aftercare
Kentucky Organ Donor Affiliates

Not a Wasted Breath is an amazing story of courage, hope and the heartache that is cystic fibrosis. Todd's zest for life was—and still is—inspiring to all of us who work hard every day to find a cure and/or control for this disease. I look forward to the day when CF stands for Cure Found.

—Beth Mattingly Denham, MPA, CFRM
Executive Director KY/WV Chapter
Cystic Fibrosis Foundation

NOT A WASTED
BREATH

I hope you will be inspired by
Todd's deep faith and zest for life.

LaRecea Gibbs
larecea @ nctc.com

NOT A WASTED BREATH

Living Fearlessly with
Cystic Fibrosis

LaRecea Tabor Gibbs

TATE PUBLISHING & *Enterprises*

Published by Tate Publishing & Enterprises, LLC
127 E. Trade Center Terrace | Mustang, Oklahoma 73064 USA
1.888.361.9473 | www.tatepublishing.com

Tate Publishing is committed to excellence in the publishing industry. The company reflects the philosophy established by the founders, based on Psalm 68:11,
"The Lord gave the word and great was the company of those who published it."

Book design copyright © 2010 by Tate Publishing, LLC. All rights reserved.
Cover design by Blake Brasor
Interior design by Joey Garrett

Published in the United States of America

ISBN: 978-1-61663-935-8
1. Biography & Autobiography / General
2. Health & Fitness / Diseases / General
10.09.14

DEDICATION

To the memory of Ernest Todd Gibbs, my son, my friend, my teacher and to my daughters, Angela Martin and Hope Turner Cummiskey, whose unconditional love and support for Todd helped him achieve amazing accomplishments.

ACKNOWLEDGMENTS

Many persons supported and encouraged Todd during his thirty-one year journey of life. Just as they did in his life, many people are responsible for encouraging and supporting me and contributing to the telling of the story of that journey. Without their help, this book would have remained Todd's unfinished dream. I want to first thank and acknowledge each person who wrote a tribute or shared a memory for this book. Each one represents different areas and periods of Todd's life, and I am not only grateful for their contributions to this book, but also thankful for the impact they had on his life: Dr. Dero Downing, Jeff Younglove, Ken Goforth, David Young, Rev. Donnie Meador, Lana Jo Stone, Dr. Jamshed Kanga, and LaDawn Reynolds. Thanks to the citizens of Allen County for always supporting Todd. To each teacher who touched Todd's life, I am grateful. To the nurses, therapists, and doctors at the University of Kentucky, I give my thanks. As Todd often stated, you are the best. A special thanks to CF doctors, Dr. David Wilson and Dr. Jamshed Kanga. I am forever indebted to you. Thanks to Rev. Chuck Pruitt for being there for Todd at every crisis, even without our calling. Thanks to Shirley Fleming, Susan Raby, and Rosemary and Rodney Parsons, the best friends for whom a person could hope. You have always been there with an ear to listen and a shoulder on which to lean. Todd's story would not have been told without the support and encouragement of Janey Hays, Kathleen Knapp, Joey Garrett and Blake Brasor at Tate Publishers. Janey believed in my book from the beginning, Kathleen encouraged me until the end, and Joey and Blake brought it life with their designs.

I am grateful to Marion and Melissa Napier for typing Todd's journal and Cary Morris for answering my numerous computer questions and to my parents, the late Aubrey and Lois Tabor, who taught me, by example, that with God's help, one could face any adversity. Thanks to the following that gave their time to read my manuscript and made suggestions or gave endorsements: John Hagaman, Sandy Hickey, Beth Mattingly, H. David Wilson, Shirley Fleming, and Cheryl Sheppard. Thanks to my daughters for their contributions to this book: Angela Martin for writing the Foreword and Hope Turner Cummiskey for suggesting the title *Not a Wasted Breath*. Thanks to my sons-in-law, Craig Martin and Patrick Cummiskey, for sharing my life. Last, but usually first in my heart and life, a special recognition of gratitude goes to my grandchildren, Calister, Alex, and Will Turner, Connor Martin, and Jackson and Ansley Cummiskey. I hope as you grow, Todd's life becomes an inspiration to you. I want this book to help you better know the uncle whom you never had the opportunity to meet.

TABLE OF CONTENTS

Part III—Todd's Journey through the Eyes of His Community

FOREWORD

A SISTER REMEMBERS
ANGELA GIBBS MARTIN

How do you find the words to describe your lifelong hero? Quite simply, Todd was the most amazing, accomplished, funny, hard-working, courageous, and spiritual individual I have ever known. To me, he was a father figure. To the rest of the world, he was my big brother.

Adjectives alone are inadequate to describe Todd's larger-than-life personality and the impact his life had on others. Quite simply, Todd was like a campfire. People gravitated to him, because Todd enveloped everyone in warmth, friendship, light, and laughter. Around Todd, stories were told, retold, and always embellished with humor and ringing with laughter. After he died, for those who knew and loved him, the world became infinitely darker, colder, and quieter. His life was so bright, that when it was extinguished, many of us who loved him felt lost and adrift. Yet, Todd's light shown so brightly, that even in death, it continues to guide and inspire.

Todd approached life by embracing Horace's phase in his Latin poem, *Idyllium de rosis:* "Carpe diem." However, Todd cared far less for Horace's version than the same sentiment expressed by the wise Captain John-Luc Picard of the starship Enterprise: "Make now, always, the most precious time. Now will never come again. Seize the day."

Oh, how my brother could seize a day! The amount of activities Todd could cram into a single day will forever inspire and confound me. Just listening to him catalog his days was enough to leave me exhausted. It wasn't *what* he accomplished that was so inspirational, it was *how* he did them that always left me humbled. Todd never did anything half way. He gave everything he did all his energy, passion, and enthusiasm and could make even the most mundane task *fun!* Todd felt that the basic ingredient to life was a generous dose of hilarity.

Another of Todd's traits I admired was his approach to life's obstacles. It wasn't that he avoided or ignored them. Rather, Todd felt that obstacles were one of God's ways of telling him that he was headed in the wrong direction and there were other, better paths to pursue that would yield even greater rewards.

For example, one of my brother's great loves was basketball, but at 5'4" [and he lied about his height], Todd was not exactly NBA material. Instead of giving up and staying on the sidelines, Todd chose other paths. He became a trainer for the high school basketball team. He helped create and manage a successful high school girls' basketball tournament. He coached several Little League girls' basketball teams, and he became an accredited high school basketball referee.

The memory of watching a man with only thirty percent lung capacity running up and down a basketball court with young, healthy kids always inspired me and others. To this day, I still have young women who occasionally remind me that Todd was their Little League coach and share how he positively affected their lives. In a way, Todd touched more lives by *not* playing basketball than he ever would have had he been physically able to play the sport.

Was my big brother perfect? Of course, not! After all, what brother who shoots his sister [me, of course] with a BB gun for target practice can be portrayed fairly as perfect? He was human, after all, with human failings. [And, unfortunately for me, a very good aim!]

As much as it pains me to admit it, as a child Todd could be cunningly deceptive. A case in point was the Santa Conspiracy that he instigated in the late seventies. My parents decided it was time to explain to my younger sister, Hope, the *truth* about Santa. Todd feared that with the youngest kid in the household *"in on the secret,"* the overall quantity of Christmas presents we kids would receive would be significantly reduced. Drastic action was obviously needed.

After explaining the dire situation to Hope, he convinced her that the only way we could protect the bounty of Christmas would be if she simply refused to allow our parents to broach the Santa subject. If cornered, she should convince our parents that, like Tom Cruise in the movie, "A Few Good Men," she simply couldn't "handle the truth."

Hope, for her part, took to the role like a fish to water. My parents were baffled at Hope's hysterical reaction whenever they tried to have the "Santa talk" with her. She would cry. She would pretend innocence. She would run screaming from the room with hands over her ears repeating, "I still believe! I still believe!" Truly, her performances were Oscar-worthy. Of course, she had an excellent director and co-conspirator in my brother. This scene continued for *two* Christmases! It wasn't until our parents seriously began contemplating seeking professional help for her that we [by this time, I was an accessory after the fact] came clean and admitted the nefarious plan.

So perfect, Todd was not. However, for all his tricks and ploys, [and he was full of them] he was the best big brother a sister could ever have. I miss his presence, wisdom, laughter, and love on a daily basis. I also miss his protection. For my sister and me, Todd was a human version of Lassie: protecting us from harm, watching over us, keeping us in line, getting us out of trouble, and always being there for us. He was our best friend.

When I bought my first home in my mid-twenties, Todd showed up to inspect the locks on the doors and to give me some unusual housewarming gifts. He brought batteries for the smoke detectors [which he promptly installed] and a fire extinguisher, which he insisted I keep in my kitchen. Why? Because, he sincerely warned, "With your cooking, Sis, I don't want you taking any chances."

Todd's desire to protect loved-ones didn't stop even when he was facing imminent death. In my last conversations with him, never once did he complain, express fear, anger, or any of the other emotions I know he had to be experiencing. That was just Todd. While he couldn't protect those he loved from the pain of his eventual death, he was determined to shield us from experiencing his fear, uncertainty, loneliness, and the pain of his dying. It was his last gift to me.

There are many ways to judge the worth and character of a man. One is how he *lives* his life; another is how he *leaves* this life. It takes a strong man to live fearlessly. It takes a stronger man to set aside his own fears in order to make his death easier for those he's leaving behind. And what a courageous battle with death he fought!

For these reasons, and so many more, my mother has written this book. She wanted to illustrate the great fortitude, faith, hopefulness, generosity, and strength of character that Todd demonstrated in life and death.

I will leave you with this final insight into my brother's character as it illustrates not only his incredible faith in God, but, also, his generosity of spirit, his loving heart, and his positive outlook on life.

I once asked Todd if he ever blamed God for giving him cystic fibrosis. I knew that I did. When I was three, I was initially misdiagnosed with CF. Growing up I felt as much guilt as relief at not having the disease. I believed that God had cured me because, unlike my brother, I lacked the strength of character and temperament to fight CF without succumbing to hopelessness and bitterness. As we grew older, I became convinced that God had spared the wrong child, and I keenly felt that it was an injustice to my brother. A few years before Todd died, I summoned enough courage to thank him for loving me in spite of being the child God spared.

Todd was incredulous. In the manner of a parent trying to explain a complicated subject to an endearing, but not too bright child, Todd explained that God had not given him CF. Bad genes had given him cystic fibrosis. *God* had given him the strength and courage to fight it. He told me that, in a way, CF was a gift, because it made him become a stronger person and better man.

Then he said, "You know, Sis, the worst CF can do is kill me. It can't stop me from living." And it didn't! My brother lived. He really, really lived; not just in spite of CF, but maybe-to some extent-because of it.

At my brother's funeral, one of my co-workers came to pay his respects. He did not know Todd very well, only through the stories I would tell and by my brother's reputation. However, he told me, that while he hurt for Todd and our family's loss, the people he felt the sorriest for were those who never knew Todd, because they were the ones who suffered the greatest loss.

Todd's favorite Bible verse was Ecclesiastes 3:1–15, which begins: "To every thing there is a season, and a time to every purpose under the heaven:" I think this book is Todd's time "to speak." It is my hope, that through it, Todd will speak to you, inspire you, and encourage you to fearlessly seize each day!

INTRODUCTION

I never planned to write a book. It was not my dream or even an item on my mostly unfinished "bucket list." It was my son, Todd's, plan and his uncompleted dream.

I have enjoyed writing since a child, but only short stories, articles, or personal reflections. I often wrote as a therapeutic tool. It was one reason I wanted to teach my students that writing could be a joy, not just a dreaded class assignment. One of my biggest thrills was receiving my first acceptance letter from a national magazine for a story I had written. But writing a book? Never!

One of my first concerns in writing this book was how to incorporate Todd's writings. Another fear was if I wrote only from my viewpoint, the reader might perceive me as a grieving mother who pictured her child as perfect and elevated her child's impact after his death. That is why I included reflections by others, so the reader could see Todd from different viewpoints and chose to divide the book into three parts.

Part I contains the chapters Todd wrote before his death. He hoped they would someday result in a book. It also contains his journal entries written from his first day on the transplant list until shortly before his death. They were his private thoughts kept only to himself. Todd never allowed his friends or family to see his fear or the depth of his pain. He kept an upbeat spirit in front of everyone. I was with him during the weekdays throughout most of his final four months, but when I first read his journal, I saw Todd from a new perspective. Since I did not want the reader to have only his thoughts as he was dying, I have also included selected articles Todd wrote for his newspaper column, *Scoop sounds off,* during his "healthy" life.

Part II contains my memories, some that were difficult and sad, but I hope the reader can still feel the joy of that life. I want this book to be a celebration of Todd's life and my pride in being his mother. This is *not* a memoriam to loss.

Part III reflects the impact Todd had on friends, community, and family. It includes different viewpoints and perspectives by people who were touched by his life. I hope it gives the reader a true picture of how sometimes an obstacle can be, in the end, a treasured gift in disguise.

It is difficult to write about the life and death of one's child. Perhaps, that is why it has taken me fourteen years to do so. I often felt that God wanted me to write this book, but I would question if it was my idea, the desire to keep my promise to Todd to help him tell his story, or really God who wanted me to show how he had worked in Todd's life.

I hope the reader is encouraged and inspired by Todd's journey. Although I felt the challenge of writing a book was far above my abilities, I have trusted God to guide me in the writing, and I hope he places it into the hands and hearts of those who can benefit from it.

LaRecea Gibbs

PROLOGUE

The bumper sticker read, "Don't take your organs to heaven. God knows we need them here." It was on the car in front of mine as I rode in the procession from Todd's funeral to his burial site.

I had been in many funeral processions before, including both parents and two brothers, but this was entirely different. Todd was my son!

We expect that someday we will face the difficult task of burying our parents. We realize, perhaps even hope, that we will outlive our siblings, but it is not the natural order of life for a parent to bury a child. It is one of life's greatest losses.

That bumper sticker had a special significance for me. Todd died five days past his thirty-first birthday while waiting for a double lung transplant. He had cystic fibrosis. [CF] We had hoped, prayed, and believed that donor lungs would be found in time to give him a future.

All Todd's life, he had fought and won many battles with CF, and he believed that new lungs would enable him to win the war. Now his war was over. I was left with battle scars in my heart that I knew would never completely heal.

I have always enjoyed reading about the miracle of a life changed because of an organ transplant. I never expected to be personally affected. I still read about and rejoice for the patients and their families who receive the gift of donation. Those stories need to be shared. Perhaps, they cause a reader to make the decision to become a donor. I want to tell the other, and sadly more common, story of the approximately eighteen persons who die each day waiting for the gift that never comes.

This is one of those stories. It expresses the heartbreak of a mother whose son is dying and whose only hope is a transplant. It tells the impact his life had on his friends and community. More importantly, it gives insight into a young man's feelings and thoughts as he hopes, waits, prays, waits, believes, waits, waits, waits…

When Todd was placed on the national list for a lung transplant in June of '95, he searched for articles that would help him prepare for what lay ahead. Everything he found was written from the medical point of view. Todd wanted something from a patient's perspective. Nothing was available, so he decided he would use the recovery time from his surgery to write the story of his journey.

In order to prepare for the book he hoped to write, he kept a daily journal from the day he was placed on the list until shortly before his death, Friday the 13, October 1995. I promised Todd I would help him tell his story, but we had expected it to have the fairy tale ending of "and they lived happily ever after."

This is the story of a man who faced many obstacles. This is not just a story about cystic fibrosis or waiting for a transplant. It is for anyone who has faced, is now facing, or will someday face a life-changing obstacle. Cystic fibrosis was never the focus of Todd's life. Todd did not intend for his book to focus on CF, waiting for a transplant, or even living with a chronic illness. Todd told me that he wanted to tell his story to show how, in spite of any obstacle a person might face, with faith, determination, hard work, and a sense of humor, one could overcome anything. That was Todd's recipe for life. It was not spoken. It was not written in some sacred place. It was the way he lived his life.

Note: I invited Todd's widow to contribute a reflection or memory. She declined and asked that I not use her picture or mention her name in this book. However, it is impossible to tell Todd's story without sharing that he was married. I will respect her privacy and will refer to her as Sarah.

PART I
TODD'S JOURNEY
THROUGH HIS EYES

Note: This section contains Todd's journal entries written from his first day on the organ transplant list until shortly before his death. He wrote the first four chapters hoping they would become part of a book he intended to write during his recovery after receiving his new lungs. He kept the daily journal entries to remind himself of his feelings during the waiting period so his book would be more accurate. I have also included several articles he wrote weekly for our local newspaper, Scoop sounds off. They reflect his attitude, character, views, and often his humor that I feel will give the reader a better look into the essence of the Todd we all knew for thirty-one years. Some are in Part I, and others are located in Part II when I felt they were pertinent.

MY LIFE

Imagine the doctors telling you that, at your current rate of progression, you have less than a year to live. Then they explain a procedure that, if successful, could give you a long life free of many of the life-threatening health problems you have faced all your life. The only problems are the procedure is risky, expensive, and it depends upon the unfortunate death of a stranger and the compassion and love from its family to give you the gift of life.

I have always known that I had a fatal disease, a disease that was trying to keep me from taking the very breath needed for life. I could accept that. However, I also knew that if I let it control my life and dwelled on it, then in essence it would have already won. That, I could *never* accept.

When I was five, doctors told my family I had cystic fibrosis, the nation's most common genetic killer. CF is always fatal, one hundred percent of the time, and there is no cure. The doctors explained to my parents that I would never live a normal life and would probably die before reaching my teenage years.

They were wrong. Today, I work in University Relations at Western Kentucky University where I graduated in 1994. I am director of Kentucky's largest invitational girls' basketball tournament, a city council member for Scottsville, KY, and married to a wonderful young woman. Most importantly, I am thirty years old. The doctors were wrong.

I have always thought I had to prove to everyone that cystic fibrosis does not control me. I control it. Most of the time that works. The doctors told my family that I would not be able to attend public school, so I graduated and went to college. They said it would be difficult for me to play any sport. That is why I fought hard and finally made my Little League All-Star baseball team. I was told playing basketball [being a true Kentuckian, it is my favorite sport] was out of the question. This time they were right. I am too small at 5'4," so I did the next best thing and became a high school basketball referee. Every time I was told about something I could not do, it made me more determined to do it. However, it has not always been a smooth road—far from it.

Over the past thirty years, there have been more than eighty hospitalizations relating to complications with CF. Few have been under ten days while some have been longer than a month. Some were routine while others were more serious. During one hospitalization, when I was eighteen, my doctor told me I had a week to live, and there was nothing else she could do. Good thing I never listen to my doctors.

Each hospitalization has taught me a little about myself and a lot about others. Some of my best, most special friendships are from relationships started during hospitalizations at the University of Kentucky Medical Center. They involve patients, nurses, respiratory therapists, and doctors. Different people from different walks of life. All were drawn together by a common bond: cystic fibrosis.

My friendships with other CF patients have been the most special. We stayed up late at night and talked about things that we could not discuss with anyone else, our hopes and fears about CF. We knew how the other felt when we had to put our lives on hold for an unexpected and unwanted hospitalization.

We knew of each other's fears. Would this be the time that the antibiotics would fail and the disease would win? Often, it did. Over a two-year period, I lost five friends with CF. Two of my best friends died on the same day. It is those times that I realize how serious this disease is about winning. However, I am also just as serious about winning. When I met with the last of my friends that died, Julie told me it was up to me to beat this disease. I plan to take her advice.

LaRecea Gibbs

Ecclesiastes tells us, "To everything there is a season, and a time for every purpose under the heaven: A time to be born and a time to die." It is my favorite verse of the Bible, because it covers all aspects of life. I have never questioned why I have CF, although I sometimes wonder why I am alive and my friends are not.

I read this verse and I understand that God did not give me a fatal disease, but he can help me use it to help others. CF has given me a unique outlook on life. It has made me appreciate each moment, special friendships, and even the hardships. I have always believed it is the difficult times that make us appreciate the good times. CF has done that.

CF has also helped solidify my relationship with God. There have been so many nights, especially alone in the hospital, that he comforted me to sleep. It was he who told me that things were all right. CF was not going to win this fight. It was he that shared in my victories each time I left the hospital, proving the "human spirit and prayer are more powerful than any drug."

If I had the choice of doing life over again without CF, knowing then what I know now, I would not. Whether I like it or not, CF is a very important part of me. If I changed CF, I would change my whole being. I would change friendships and life experiences. I would not know Dr. Kanga, the Parsons, [parents of a friend, Roddy, whom he met in the hospital, who had received a kidney transplant] LaDawn, [a respiratory therapist] Lisa, [a UK nurse] and countless others who are a very important part of my being.

There is more to life than health. It is said, "If you have your health, you have everything." I cannot agree with that statement. Life is friendships, love, relationships, and experiences. If you change the fact that I have CF, you change my whole world, all that I am and have been. That, I am not willing to do.

Life cannot be measured in quantity but in quality. I do not feel sorry for someone who dies young, but lived a full and happy life giving more to others than they are willing to take in return.

I feel sorry for someone old that has always been healthy, but unhappy, and wanted more than they are willing to give.

I know someday soon researchers will find a cure for CF, but my fight cannot wait. A lung transplant will do what researchers have not been able to—cure my lungs from an enemy invader. Perhaps, I will finally be able to beat this disease, just as Julie wanted.

WAITING FOR "THE GIFT"

These lungs have been a part of me for more than thirty years, giving me the air needed to sustain life. These same lungs are now trying to kill me, forcing me to make the decision to remove them from my body. It is the only hope I have to save my life.

For twenty-five years, I had proven the doctors wrong. I had done everything they told me I could not do. I had graduated from high school, college, worked numerous jobs, refereed basketball games, been elected to my city's council, and had gotten married. I had pushed my lungs to the limit in an effort to prove that I was stronger than cystic fibrosis ever thought about being. However, here I sat in a hospital room, waiting for someone to die, so that I might have their lungs to live. It was one final effort to beat the disease I have been fighting all my life. Although my body will still have cystic fibrosis, my new lungs will not, a moral victory. I always said CF would not kill me … this was going to prove me right.

It was in 1987 that Dr. Kanga first mentioned a lung transplant. A good CF friend of mine, Jack Girvin, and I were hospitalized together. One night, Dr. Kanga discussed our futures and the course of treatment that we wanted. He talked with us about which life-sustaining measures we wanted him to take when the disease was in its final stages. We talked about painkillers, respirators, and intensive care treatment. He also talked with us concerning at what point we wanted him to stop and let the natural course of death take place. Amid all of the discussion, he mentioned a lung transplant. It was something new that was being done. Not on CF patients, but it was possible for the future. Jack and I both agreed we were interested in the prospect, neither really believing that our conditions would ever warrant such a drastic procedure.

Jack and I were about the same age. Our lifestyles had been similar—very active with brief hospitalizations to offset infections. In fact, Jack's health had always been much better than mine. I had been hospitalized at UK dozens of times while Jack had only recently been sick enough to require admissions. Our friendship grew as our hospitalizations increased. It was easy for us to talk with each other. We both had similar dreams for the future, and we both faced the same obstacles in reaching those dreams. We spent hours and hours during those long nights talking. Hospitalizations can be lonely times. Hours seem to drag into days. When you are a teenager, those days seem like wasted times that can never be regained. We tried passing the time talking about girls, movies, school, work, marriage, cystic fibrosis and how we would beat CF.

During our hospitalizations, we had other young adult friends with CF. There were several of us that became a close group. We formed support groups and visited and called each other when we were at the Medical Center. We kept up with each other's health conditions as a mother does her own children. We knew when one of us had been hospitalized for a routine check-up or if it was something more serious. At the center of our group was our father, Dr. Kanga. Our relationships with Kanga would be difficult to describe. He is more than a doctor; he is a friend. He was also a groomsman in my wedding. I know he crosses the patient-doctor friendship line, but who cares. That is why he is such a great doctor. His treatment comes from his heart as well as his head. We always knew he was doing what he thought was best for us.

As my condition remained the same, and in some cases actually improved, my friends' did not. Over a two-year period between 1989 and 1991, I watched them die one by one. My two closest friends died on the same day in 1989. One of them was Jack. For the first time in my life, I realized the impact this disease could have on the body. I also realized there might be a day when CF decided to escalate the war on my body. I just wondered if there would be an option when that day came. The answers came to both those questions in early 1995, less than ten years after Kanga first uttered the words "lung transplant" to me.

I took Jack's death very hard. I attended Jack's funeral one day and another friend's funeral the next day. For weeks, I had trouble sleeping and slept on my couch for more than a month following their deaths.

SCOOP SOUNDS OFF—

THE DEATHS OF TWO
FRIENDS THE SAME DAY

Note: Todd wrote a weekly column for a local newspaper, The Allen County News, called "Scoop sounds off." They are reprinted with permission of Mike Patton, Editor. Todd wrote the following article about Jack and Melissa the week after their deaths.

She was sixteen when we met. He was eighteen. We all three had a lot in common. We liked Kentucky basketball. We had big hopes and dreams for the future. And we all had cystic fibrosis. CF is a genetic disorder that affects the mucus producing glands of the body. It most commonly affects the lungs in the form of infections. There is no cure. It is fatal.

Melissa, Jack, and I all met while we were in the University of Kentucky Medical Center. It is a strange place to make friends, but over the past twenty years, some of my best friendships have started at UK. We all knew that CF was fatal, and we often talked about it, but we never planned on it.

It was a year ago this week that I faced the most difficult day of my life. That one day has changed the way I look at life.

My doctor, Jamshed Kanga, in Lexington, called and told me that Jack was very ill and was not expected to recover. He also said Melissa was in the hospital, but was doing better and would probably go home soon. I called and talked with both. The conversation with Jack was unusual. We both knew what was happening, and we talked about everything in the world...except

CF. But, we both knew what was on our minds. We said goodbye to each other, knowing it was probably the last time we would talk. When I talked to Melissa, we mostly talked about Jack. Our conversation was not as tense.

A week after we talked, Dr. Kanga's nurse, Lois, called and told me the news that I had been bracing myself to hear. Jack had died, but she told me Melissa had gone home two days earlier. It was good news and bad news at the same time.

Two hours later, Dr. Kanga called and told me something for which I had not braced myself. Melissa had died.

CF had won twice in the same day. Losing one friend is hard enough, but when you lose two friends on the same day, it is overwhelming.

Up to this point in life, I had been able to face everything with a sense of humor. Suddenly, life wasn't funny anymore.

It was through a third friend that I was able to get back the right perspective on life. Julie is twenty-one, and in February, I got a call from Lexington that she was very ill. I was asked to talk with her and help her face what was happening, but a funny thing happened while I was talking to her. She told me not to give up. She said it was up to me to keep fighting and beat this disease. The tables were turned. Instead of me helping her face death, she was helping me accept the loss of Jack and Melissa.

The doctors were wrong, and Julie made a remarkable recovery. She's back at home now and is doing better, but I'll never forget our talk. She helped me realize to live life for what it is, a gift. If we think about death, then we fail to live life.

Suddenly, major problems don't seem so important. The grass is a little greener; the sky is a little bluer; and life seems a little simpler. Life goes on.

A year after they died, it's time to let go. A song by Linda Ronstadt says it best. It goes: "Goodbye my friend, I know I'll never see you again, but the times together through all the years, will take away these tears. I'm okay now...Goodbye my Friend(s)..."

It's strange how it takes death to make you appreciate life. Thanks Julie.

Jack and Melissa, it's okay now. Goodbye, my friends; I'll still miss you...

[Exactly one year to the date of Jack and Melissa's deaths and the week this column was published, Julie died.]

CHILDHOOD MEMORIES

I have always known I had cystic fibrosis. My mother and father were always very honest and open with me. CF was no big deal. It was simply a part of my life in which I had no control. But I was determined, at a very early age, not to let it control me.

Up to the point of my diagnosis, my health problems had been blamed on numerous problems ranging from asthma to allergies. It was a doctor in Nashville, TN that finally confirmed that I had CF.

CF is a genetically inherited disease passed on by both parents. The treatments were crude, ineffective, and time consuming when I was diagnosed. They ranged from sleeping in a mist tent that left the child soaking wet by morning, to consuming foul tasting liquids in an effort to break up the mucus in the stomach. The doctors also confirmed my parents' worst fear. The disease they passed on was always fatal. The life expectancy was age twelve.

Luckily, for me, my parents decided it was the quality of life and not the quantity that mattered. I lived and was treated as if I did not have a fatal illness. They didn't give me any and everything I wanted. I attended school and did what other children did. I played baseball. I played basketball. I went out in the rain and I played in the snow. Other CF parents shuddered when they found out how lax my parents were. My parents did the CF treatments like the doctors ordered, but they also let me be a kid growing up in the hills of Kentucky. Some other parents were keeping their children at home, requiring home education if anything at all.

They never let them out in the rain and the snow was completely off limits. They gave their child motorcycles and all the toys they would ever want. After all, they had CF and would not live to be twelve. Most did not, except for the one that had the parents that let their child live a normal life. He was still alive at twelve and still going strong.

I think of my childhood as normal. I am always careful about using the word *normal.* Just because you have a disease, does not mean you are not normal. It just makes you different. I have always considered myself different. That is the way I like it.

I grew up on a small farm near Scottsville, Kentucky. My house was only a few miles from the Tennessee state line, which is about one hundred sixty miles from the University of Kentucky Medical Center, my CF headquarters in times of crisis. I lived on the farm with my mother and father and two younger sisters. All of our neighbors were close friends or relatives making it a very close-knit community. I had a wonderful childhood. I loved living on the farm, being outdoors. On the farm, I could be like any other kid. I would take off early in the morning and sometimes stay gone all day wandering in the woods, exploring the fields, or playing by the ponds and lakes. I mowed the grass and kept my room clean.

Our church was the center of the community. Most of the people that attended were relatives and all were friends. Some of my fondest memories revolve around the Holland Baptist Church. I remember dinner and singing on the grounds. I remember those hot summer days when the voice of our pastor would echo against the walls and wooden floors of the old structure. His voice was bold and strong and commanded a young person's attention and respect.

It was in that small country church that the basis of my spiritual growth was established. It was there I learned of God's love for me and my love for him. It was there that I realized that I was different in some special way and that God had a special plan for

LaRecea Gibbs

me. It was there that I committed my life to God and became a Christian in 1976. I watched my grandparents. They were there every time the door opened, no matter what. No one ever questioned their faith and love for God. It was as solid as the church foundation itself.

Holland was a small community. It was eight miles from the nearest city and was really just a spot in the crossroads, but it had a bank, a post office, a grocery, and a gas station. It was where you went to get a mid-day sandwich or grab a Coke and talk with your neighbors at the store.

The small country grocery was my favorite place. It was not just a place to purchase items. It was a place to visit, eat, and kill time. Farmers would gather to talk about the crops. Housewives would catch up on the community news while we would wander around barefoot on the black oil-stained floors looking at the candy and ice cream. It was a place where you could say, "Charge it," and they would. It was a place you always knew you were welcome.

Another key community gathering point was the Community Center. It was located close to our house across the field. It was where the annual fish fry and Halloween parties were held. It was where my dad would disappear for his Lion's Club meetings.

We did not grow up rich. In fact, some people might consider us poor. But we always had what we needed, and I consider my childhood a very rich experience. At home, I did not get any more attention than my two sisters, Angela and Hope. We were all treated the same.

In public, it was a different matter. I was always having newspapers, radio stations, and television crews doing stories on the "rural Kentucky boy that is living longer than he should." They viewed me as the tough fighter that never gave up and fought hard on a daily basis to defeat his crippling disease.

My home family saw another side of the story…a loving, kind brother one minute that would carry his sister up a hill after she fell down, or a mean, vindictive brother that shot his sister with a BB gun. At home, I was normal. That was the way I wanted to be in public.

That is why my public image has always been very important to me. I know people are going to think what they want, but actions can feed positive or negative images to those thoughts. I never wanted to look sick, so I would go to extremes to keep from it. I would study the actions of other CF patients and try to sit in positions they did not in an effort to help me look stronger. I would try to walk taller, talk slower, and breathe deeper. In the hospital, I would try to spend most of my time sitting in a chair instead of a bed and making rounds with Dr. Kanga, so he could show parents of the *sick kids* what a healthy CF patient looks like. It also showed them you could live a productive life with this deadly disease. It made Kanga feel good about his accomplishments. It made the parents more optimistic about the future, and it made me feel that I was above everyone else with this disease. I was winning and was always going to beat this disease. That is what I had in mind. Cystic fibrosis had something else it intended to do.

WAITING

"Always make now the most precious time, because now will never come again." That phrase came from a Star Trek show I was watching one night while hospitalized at the University of Kentucky Medical Center. Now that I am waiting for a lung transplant, its meaning takes on a new significance.

It is difficult to describe the feeling when you hear the doctor say you have six months to a year to live. Your world goes numb. The past stands still and the future simply vanishes. Everyone has probably once thought, "What would I do if I only had one year to live? Where would I go? Who would I see?" These were questions I had casually thought of in the past, but they weren't serious thoughts until it was really happening to me. I was too sick to travel. My daily activities centered on being able to walk back and forth from room to room. Going out visiting friends was difficult because of the constant oxygen I was taking. I had become uncomfortable around other people because of my physical condition and appearance. I was at an all time low in my life. It suddenly seemed unimportant and useless. I lost my focus, my determination, my drive. I lost the advantages of the very things that had allowed me to beat CF for thirty years, my attitude and determination.

JOURNAL ENTRY: JUNE 18, 1995

TRANSPLANT HOSPITALIZATIONS:

SUNDAY, JUNE 18, 1995

This is not the way we were supposed to spend our six-month anniversary. We sat holding each other and crying. It was time for another hospitalization, the second since our wedding six months ago. In the past, I had been averaging one hospitalization a year, but those days were gone. CF was becoming more and more determined and more and more successful at accomplishing its goal, but I was just as determined.

Over the past few weeks, my breathing had been getting progressively worse. Everyday activities were more and more difficult, and I had been missing work for the first time in my life. I avoided stairs as if they were the Ebola virus. I avoided walking at any cost, taking shortcuts or avoiding the walk all together. Even simple activities like taking a shower, sleeping, and eating took more out of me. It is alarming the rate this disease can progress.

I can look at two recent events as the start of my serious problems. In August of 1993, I fought a bout of kidney stones that left my body in a weakened state for more than two months. That was a prime time for the cystic fibrosis to strike. The other incident occurred in September of 1994 during a medication dispute with my insurance company. Those two incidents together were more than my lungs have been able to handle. For the first time in my life, the CF has gained an upper hand for the moment.

It is incredible how your priorities change. Two years ago, I was refereeing four basketball games a week, attending college full-time, working jobs at a bank, University Relations, and city councilman and still playing music for high school dances. Now I try to walk to the bathroom by myself and get back to bed before my oxygen supply runs out. Walking is more than a challenge. It is sometimes impossible. Life changes in a hurry.

The hospitalization started like many others: the same medications, the same treatments, the same routines. However, it was not the same. Three days after being admitted, my health took a turn for the worse. My breathing reached fifty times a minute with my heart pumping more than two hundred forty times during the same duration. Something was seriously wrong and, for the first time, I was about to visit the Intensive Care Unit of the University of Kentucky Medical Center.

There were certain treatments I associated with seriously ill CF patients. In the back of my mind, as long as I could avoid these treatments I was doing well. I had never used oxygen, never taken pain medicine to comfort the pain and stress of breathing, never been asked by Dr. Kanga if I wanted to be resuscitated if I stopped breathing, and never taken to ICU. That Wednesday morning, all four happened in a matter of minutes. In the back of my mind, I wondered if the fight was lost. I told Dr. Kanga I wanted to be placed on the A-R list. When he inquired what AR meant, I told him it stood for "Always Resuscitate." He agreed and it was off to Intensive Care for the first time in my life.

The move I had from my eighth floor room to the first floor Intensive Care Unit was the longest of my life. Every emotion and every fear was running through my mind. Would I get better? Would I ever be back to my usual strength? Would I be able to physically and emotionally recover from this hospitalization?

My body was wired with devices that gave vital body readings to the nurses. While this was routine, it was more wires and machines than had ever been hooked up to me at one time. Next came the pain medicine, Morphine. It was used to keep me comfortable and to help take off some of the stress of the last few hours. I was alone in a dimly lit, sterile, cold room where the only sound was the light hiss of the oxygen and the occasional warning sounds of the monitors when one of the many readings did not reach predetermined levels. Suddenly, it was more than I could take, and I broke down and cried.

I have always believed in the power of prayer. There have been many hospitalizations when I knew it was God and not the medications that got me from one day to the next. As soon as I started praying, God took over and, suddenly, I knew everything was going to be all right. I stopped crying and realized this was only a setback, the war was long from over and CF was not going to win. Soon after that, the Morphine kicked in and everything got even better. The only difference was that the Morphine stopped working after a few hours. God did not.

Those two days in Intensive Care were among the most intense and peaceful of my life. They were intense in my realization of the seriousness of my disease. They were peaceful in the time I had alone to think about my next move in defeating this disease. Cystic fibrosis may have struck a hard blow and won a battle, but the war was long from over, a war I intended on winning no matter what. That is why something as dramatic as a lung transplant went from an option to a fast reality. The time for talking was over. It was time to prepare for the most difficult part of my life and the end to my lung problems with cystic fibrosis, once and for all.

I look back at previous hospitalizations and I remember faces, not names, of nurses, doctors, roommates and others that were a very important part of my life, if only for a few days, and then were gone forever. It is incredible how many people I have met because of CF. Each taught me a little about people and a lot about myself.

Once I returned to the main floor, the preparation for a lung transplant began. Tests were taken, questions were answered, and the process was underway. It was the first time that I met the transplant team. They informed me about what I could and should expect. They were very careful that they did not overload me with too much information at one time. Each day they would explain something new. "The survival rate at UK was ninety percent." Wow, that is better than my college grades! "The heart would be stopped during the operation and all of my blood would circulate through a heart-lung machine." They assured me not to worry. The procedure was performed a dozen times a day at UK. Well, that may be true, but this situation was different. This was my heart they were stopping!

The team was very caring and very honest. It was during these conversations that I learned patients put on transplant lists usually have less than a year to live without the operation. It was the first time that I actually thought that CF was getting the upper hand. One year to live. The fight was reaching a climax and the battle lines were drawn.

Note: Todd remained in the hospital from the June 18, 1995 entry, but did not begin his daily journal entries until he was officially placed on the transplant list July 3.

LaRecea Gibbs

JOURNAL ENTRIES:
JULY 3, TO
AUGUST 27, 1995

MONDAY, JULY 3, 1995

Today, it became official. I am a lung transplant candidate. Sabrina [transplant coordinator] said that I am on the national list, and I am first on the UK list. Even though I knew it was going to happen, the realization of being on the list had a stronger impact than I expected. Sabrina took me to the Intensive Care Unit to see a transplant patient. It was uncomfortable for me. The rest of the evening was spent talking about what is ahead. I have a lot of fears, concerns, hopes and dreams. I just hope it comes while I am here and ready.

TUESDAY, JULY 4, 1995

It is a holiday and that is when many transplants take place. UK has done three over the past week. Since I am next on the list for my blood type, it is a testing time. I try not to think about it, but it dominates my thoughts.

WEDNESDAY, JULY 5, 1995

Transplant tests started today, x-rays, blood work and EKG's, etc. Doctors ordered sleeping medicine last night, and it caused me to be drowsy all day. Doctor Kanga is talking about letting me go home on Friday, but he is not completely sure I am ready. When I go home I will be on oxygen all of the time. I am not crazy about that, but I guess it is an easy tradeoff for taking care of my lungs and heart until the transplant. Maybe after a week at home, I will be able to go back to work at WKU. The story in *The Citizen Times* ran today. I hope it answers some questions people have concerning the transplant.

THURSDAY, JULY 6, 1995

The transplant team explains more and more about the operation each day. It will be a tremendous ordeal, but I am ready. I just want these old lungs out and to breathe easier. Leaving tomorrow is out of the question. Kanga wants to keep me through the weekend in case there is a transplant. Weekends and holidays are key transplant times.

FRIDAY, JULY 7, 1995

This has been a difficult week. I am nervous about going home. I had hoped everything would happen quickly, but it is not. Unless I get the transplant today, I will go home tomorrow. It has been a very difficult hospitalization. The home health agency has been to the house to set up the oxygen system. They also brought tanks to the hospital for the drive home. I have never left the hospital feeling so poorly and so weak. I just hope I continue to get better at home. I just hope it is a short trip home before we return for the transplant.

[Note: missing journal entry for Saturday, July 8]

SUNDAY JULY 9, 1995

Today I left the UK Medical Center after a three-week stay. Roddy and Melissa [Roddy's wife] met me at the hospital. It is good to have their friendship during this time. Dr. Kanga and I had a long talk about this hospitalization. It was a difficult visit.

He told me to expect a longer recovery this time. He wants me to be patient. I will try. The trip home was long and difficult. When I got home, I was not able to walk up the two steps in front of my house by myself. My legs do not work in an upward motion. My strength is zero. My new oxygen machine was waiting for me, but this will take some adjusting. It is good to be home—for how long, I do not know.

MONDAY, JULY 10. 1995

It was a good day. I was stronger than I expected. I have been moving around the house better than I expected. Bill Reece [president of a local bank, friend and groomsman at Todd's wedding] came by and we talked about writing a will and the benefits of a Living Will. I think I am going to pursue both. The Living Will would take the decision making pressure off my wife in case something went wrong. Tonight, Donnie [one of his closest friends] worked the sound system at the fair while I attended the city council meeting. Mom drove me. I am still not ready to drive and I held out well until the last few minutes. I wore my oxygen, but I feel uncomfortable with it while I am out in public. The radio story aired today. Maybe that will keep down the rumors. I slept well for first time in weeks.

Between the ages of 13 and 25: .

...I've climbed mountains at the top of the country in Alaska, and I've swum in the ocean at the bottom of the country in the Florida Keys.

...I've marched in front of millions of people in parades in Philadelphia, and I've sat alone in the Alaskan wilderness.

...I've watched grizzly bears play and killer whales swim in the wild, and I've ridden an elephant in a parade.

...I've worked as a news director of a radio station, and I've worked filling boats with gasoline on a summer job.

...I've stood where our country's constitution was written, and I've sat in the Vice President's chair in the Senate chamber where that document is carried out each day.

...I've interviewed music and movie stars, and I've been interviewed by newspapers, radio and television.

...I've been sent to the principal's office, and I've met with our President in the Oval Office.

...I've sat in giant churches in New Orleans and Philadelphia, and I've worshiped in small country churches.

All after I was 12, the doctor's predetermined life expectancy when I was diagnosed.

Between 25 and 30:

I won state and national news awards.

I graduated from college and went on to graduate school.

I got a job at a bank, at a university, at a newspaper, and at two radio stations.

I refereed a district basketball championship as the head official.

I was elected to the Scottsville City Council, twice.

I became a deacon at the Scottsville Baptist Church.

I traveled to another country for the first time.

I walked in a rain forest in Washington State.

I fished in the Atlantic Ocean and swam in the Pacific Ocean.

I've stood at military funerals in Arlington National Cemetery.

And I married a wonderful lady that changed my life forever. You can do anything you want. When someone tells you that you can't do something, prove them wrong.

The doctors said I wouldn't be able to finish grade school, so I graduated from college. The doctors said I couldn't play Little League baseball, so I made the All-Star team.

The doctors said I couldn't hold down a full-time job, so I worked fifty to sixty hours a week as a news director of a radio station.

The doctors said I couldn't play basketball. They were right I am too short. Instead, I became a Kentucky varsity basketball official.

Don't let anyone tell you what you can't do.
When you reach one goal, set another.

TUESDAY, JULY 11, 1995

I don't have as much energy today. I guess yesterday was too much. I left the house today to have my teeth cleaned at the dentist. The waiting room was full when I arrived, and I could hear people whisper about my getting a lung transplant. I did not want to wait out front with everyone looking at me, so I went to the back. Mom drove me, and I still had some trouble walking to and from the house. I had a quiet evening but did not sleep well.

WEDNESDAY, JULY 12, 1995

Today was a difficult day. My breathing was not as good today, and I had a bad chest pain and lightness attack. I went back to dentist today and saw Dr. Huntsman. Everyone is very understanding and supportive of my situation. Hope, Calister, [Hope's fiancé] Angela and Mom came over for dinner. I had a difficult day but slept some in a chair. I will be so glad to sleep normally again.

THURSDAY, JULY 13, 1995

I stayed at home all day. Mom spent most of the day with me. I am still having trouble breathing. I have tried to keep my exercise down to a minimum. I am getting very tired of waiting, and I know the wait could be just getting started. Staying at home, alone, gives me too much time to think about what is happening, but I am still too weak to leave the house.

FRIDAY, JULY 14, 1995

Still no word from UK on a transplant. With the start of the first weekend at home, the chances are greater. Dad brought his air-conditioner from his house to put in the front room. The oxygen machine makes so much heat that it is uncomfortable. Dad and Granny have been great and caring. Today, I did well. It was a fair day.

SATURDAY, JULY 15, 1995

It was a good day. Sarah and I spent the day at home and I did not try to get out. Sarah played music for a wedding dance that I scheduled before I got sick. Since many transplants occur over the weekend, we were both nervous about her being gone, even for a few short hours. Donnie helped Sarah and everything went well.

SUNDAY, JULY 16, 1995

I was not able to go to church today. I really wanted to say a few words to the church. Since I will not be able to go to church for about six months, I needed to go, but I couldn't. I felt worse in the afternoon and had to cancel our plans with Todd and Lisa. [Todd's best friend from first grade and his wife]

MONDAY, JULY 17, 1995

I received copies of my will and Living Will today. It seems like a big step but a much-needed one. I had a very good day today and got around well. Lisa [his favorite nurse whom he visited in Alaska in '93] came and visited and stayed the night. It was good to see her. We talked about the old times, about Jack and lost friends. I miss them very much. If only a transplant had been an option when they were sick, they would still be around today. I am thankful that I have an option.

TUESDAY, JULY 18, 1995

The day started well but did not end that way. Dan [director of news at Western's radio station where Todd worked] and his family brought dinner. It was good to have their company. I had a severe spell in the evening and went to bed early. I'm having more trouble breathing than usual today. I am still upset that my spiritual needs have not been met as well as my other needs. I know God is in control, and I am confident that everything will work out for the best, but it would have been nice to have my spiritual needs cared for during this time.

WEDNESDAY, JULY 19, 1995

I had more trouble breathing today, maybe my worst day so far. I am getting more and more tired each day. The waiting is becoming more and more difficult. Days seem so long, and at times, I wonder if they will ever end. The nights are sometimes worse, because I have trouble sleeping. I get up and watch television or read. I do not think about the transplant every moment, nor do I think about it every time the phone rings. Sometimes I wonder if they will ever find a lung match. I am just getting tired of feeling sick. I want to get back to normal, and I hate to use the word *normal.*

THURSDAY, JULY 20, 1995

I had a good day health wise, but it wasn't very eventful, although I did have plenty of visitors. There has still been no call from Lexington. I wonder if the call will ever occur. Each day I get less and less ready for the operation. I didn't sleep well last night, because I have been having bad dreams about the surgery. I kept waking up Sarah just because I wanted to spend time with her, and I wanted to tell her I love her.

FRIDAY, JULY 21, 1995

It is Friday. It has been a long and difficult week. Mom was great. She spent every day at my house. She is very patient at a time when I am not the best company in the world. It has been a week since I left the house, and the walls are beginning to close inward.

It just takes so much effort to go out, it is not worth it. Maybe I'll get out this weekend if I feel good. Todd and Lisa spent the evening with us. I think my illness makes Lisa uncomfortable. Maybe she is afraid that Todd's health could take the same turn someday. I understand her fears, and I understand if she wants to stay away. [Todd Hurt died in '97. He had hemophilia.]

SATURDAY, JULY 22, 1995

It was another difficult day. I decided not to go anywhere. The stress and anticipation of another weekend and the possibility of a call coming in at any time is too much. There have been so many calls and visitors. It is nice to know who your true friends are. The stress is beginning to get to Sarah and me. We sometimes argue over nothing. I am more concerned about her than I am about myself.

SUNDAY, JULY 23, 1995

I was not able to go to church today. It has been about two months since I went to church. That is a record, and one I never wanted to set. The worst part is that it could be more than six months before I can go back to church, but I know he is with me during this time. Someday I will return. I had a good day but a bad evening. I'm so tired of waiting. I started crying and we both got very emotional. We decided to pray together. We always pray at meals and at night we both say our own prayers before we go to sleep, but this was the first time we had prayed aloud together. It was a very moving and spiritual experience. I am just sad we waited six months into our marriage to do so. It will become a common occurrence from this point on.

MONDAY, JULY 24, 1995

It has been another long and difficult day. I do not seem to accomplish anything anymore. This is difficult for someone that was

LaRecea Gibbs

used to four jobs and college at the same time. I am accustomed to having something to do every minute of every day. Now hours run into days and days into weeks. It is having an effect on my attitude and my outlook on life. I look at myself and see a shell of the man I used to be. I can hardly look at myself in the mirror, and I know it is difficult for my loved ones to look at me without being upset. I have to get my act together. I have to try to work hard and rebound. It could be months before I get the call. I have to work harder at getting back to a semi-normal lifestyle. If I do not, my post-opt transplant attitude could affect my recovery.

TUESDAY, JULY 25, 1995

Every day I wake up, see the sun, and feel disappointment that I slept through another night without getting a phone call from UK. My emotions sway from hour to hour, but they get more unstable each day. I cry for no reason or when something hits home. I saw a report tonight on "911" of a young child waiting for a heart transplant. It had a happy ending. He got the heart, but it showed the donor's family, and it made me cry for them. I want my lungs, but I do not want someone to die. The problem is, it is impossible to have the best of both worlds. My breathing seems worse today. I am doing my treatments like clockwork, but they do not always seem to help. I long for the days I went to work with Sarah. I dream of the days we would simply sit on the couch and snuggle. I want those days back. I need those days back. I try to have faith and be optimistic, but it gets more and more difficult. I have to get hold of the situation. God, *please* let it happen soon.

WEDNESDAY, JULY 26, 1995

It has been another difficult day, both mentally and physically. I think about Mom after her accident. [I was in a head-on car wreck with an eighteen-wheeler. The eighteen-wheeler won! After several weeks on life support and almost thirty hours of surgery on my arm, I had to retire from teaching.] All of those days she stayed at her house recovering, alone. I was not there for her as she has been there for me. I understand what she went through, and I am sorry I was not more understanding and supportive. I talked with Lois [Dr. Kanga's nurse] today. She could tell by my voice that I am not myself. She is more concerned about my mental state than my physical state, and I am too. She said I am to start cutting back on the Morphine, so I do not get addicted. I do not want to, but I know it is for the best. I have to push myself more. Today, I rode a mile and a half on my bike. Tonight, Sarah and I drove to Bowling Green [KY] around midnight. It was the first time I had been outside the house in almost two weeks. At first, I was very nervous, but I settled down and enjoyed the ride. We got doughnuts and drove around the WKU campus. The buildings always look alone and majestic at night. We drove by the Liberty church cemetery to visit Mamie's grave. Maybe this was a turning point in my recovery. At least I hope so. We will find out tomorrow.

THURSDAY, JULY 27, 1995

Still no call and no progress today. Kanga and Sabrina are on vacation through Monday, and it looks like they will be back before I get the call, if I ever get the call. Today was the worst day since I have been home. I had no energy, zero. I slept most of the day and did not see any of the visitors that came. I took a bath tonight, and it took me more than an hour. I have lost all of my dignity. I feel like God has forgotten or is mad at me. I know it is wrong and not true, but I pray and pray and nothing happens. I am just impatient and tired of hurting and not being able to breath. I need the call soon, badly. Mom's pastor came by today, but I was sleeping. Brother Pruitt is coming back tomorrow. At least I will finally have a minister to talk to about how I am feeling. The problem is that I'm not sure how I am feeling. Confused. Impatient. Anxious. Hurt. Mad. Sad. Ashamed. Excited. More emotions than I know how to describe.

FRIDAY, JULY 28, 1995

Today was an extremely bad day. My morning began with a breathing attack, and it got worse from there. The home health agency stopped by to record oxygen saturations this morning. With four liters, the readings were ninety-two percent, but they fell suddenly when the oxygen was removed. After my breathing continued to get worse, I called Lexington and another hospitalization was scheduled. I have tried to get better, but I just cannot. In the afternoon, Brother Chuck Pruitt came to visit and stayed until we left for Lexington. We talked a little about the illness and God. It was the first time anyone had taken time to talk to me about my religious feelings concerning the situation. It felt good to talk through my feelings. It was difficult leaving home. I am not sure when I will be back. I do not want to leave. I want to stay home with my wife and be her husband. I pray my transplant comes while I am here. *Please*, God.

SATURDAY, JULY 29, 1995

I had another bad attack this morning. It was bad enough the words "respirator" and "Intensive Care" were mentioned again. I do not know what to do. I try to get better, but I have no energy. The afternoon was better. Dr. Mike Anstead [Kanga's assistant] started Morphine, and that is helping my breathing. I am able to rest at night. I am still very emotional, and I am not happy about being back at UK only three weeks after leaving. This is not a good sign.

[Note: missing journal entry for Sunday, July 30.]

MONDAY, JULY 31, 1995

It has been one month since I was placed on the transplant list. This has been the longest and worst month of my life. I hope it gets easier from this point on. I am not sure how much longer I can hold out if it does not. Sarah went back to work today. It is so much harder without her. It will be Friday before she gets back. Mom is staying during the week, and Sarah will be here on weekends. Dr. Anstead said my lab reports show I am sensitive to several different drug combinations. That is good news for a change. He also said there are two new drugs that he will test to see how they work against my infections. They would be used after the transplant as a new drug treatment. I am trying to go longer and longer between Morphine doses. I do not want to become dependent, but I want to be comfortable during this time. It looks like I am here for two to three weeks unless the lungs are found while I am here. I can only hope and pray that happens.

TUESDAY, AUGUST 1, 1995

Today begins a new month. I hope and pray it is better than last month. I can honestly say that July 1995, was probably the most difficult month of my life, health wise. It is definitely one that I do not wish to live again. The summer is speeding along, and I am getting left behind; three weeks in the hospital, three weeks at home, then back to the hospital. I had so many plans for our first summer as a married couple; romantic weekend getaways, Sunday afternoon fishing trips on the lake, or quiet picnics near the creek at the farm. I did not expect it to consist of weekends worrying about IV's and medications, late night walks along the halls at UK, and hours spent talking about how we will react when we get the call that the lungs are ready and waiting for their new host. Kanga is back today, and he seemed pleased with the way I am doing. Two other transplant patients, Tandy and Billy Jo, came by to see me today. They looked well and were very encouraging. Billy Jo waited three months while Tandy waited about three hours for his transplant. I hope I am somewhere in the middle. Tests show I am sensitive to most medications, so they are being adjusted. I had lots of company today, but I was very sleepy. Mom visited with guests in the other room while I rested. I had a good talk with Lois about my concerns and feelings. She has been very helpful and a good friend.

WEDNESDAY, AUGUST 2, 1995

It is day five of this hospitalization. I slept most of the morning and all night, but only because of the medicine I get at night. I am going to try to sleep without it tonight and see if I have a better day tomorrow. I got up and walked today, but still get short of breath easily. I have noticed my breathing is better than when I was first admitted. Maybe this hospitalization will help make me stronger. Maybe that is why I am still waiting. Mostly it was an uneventful, boring day in the hospital.

THURSDAY, AUGUST 3, 1995

It is day six of this hospitalization. My day started off well but made a dramatic turn for the worse. The problems started while I was taking a shower. I was sitting down but still having trouble, because I am so weak and not breathing well. I had to stop twice and just sit in the shower. It took forty-five minutes to take a simple shower. Something that was once a routine is now a major effort. When I got out, my pulse was still above one hundred fifty, and my oxygen level was in the low eighties. I had my oxygen on the entire time. I had to increase the Morphine in the afternoon and finally got some rest. I cannot believe that a thirty-year old has to have his mom stay with him in the hospital. The WKU President's office [Dr. Thomas Meredith] sent me a WKU hat, Big Red [the school mascot] doll and other items to cheer up my room. It was a nice gift.

FRIDAY, AUGUST 4, 1995

I slept most of the day. Yesterday's effects are still having an impact on how I feel. I used more Morphine today to ease my pain so I can rest. It worked, but I still do not want to become too dependent on the painkillers. I will start trying to cut back this weekend. Dad and Granny surprised me by visiting tonight. Dad seems concerned and, as usual, is very nervous around the hospital. Granny brought food and tomatoes for everyone. I had another long sleepless night, but I am sleeping some during the day.

SATURDAY, AUGUST 5, 1995

Today starts the second week of this hospitalization and another lost summer weekend. Oh well, after the transplant we will have many more weekends to celebrate. I am not looking at these weekends being lost forever, just investment weekends for the future. I had a very good day today, my best day yet. I sat in the living room area for more than four hours visiting with Hope, Lisa, and Yvette. [Classmates of Hope who were very close to Todd] I have lost so much muscle tone and body weight that I do not like anyone seeing me like this. I have lost more than fifteen pounds over the past six months. Today I weighed ninety-eight pounds. I kept thinking of "the ninety-eight pound weakling." I just have to be confident that this is only temporary … soon the real Todd will return, hopefully.

SUNDAY, AUGUST 6, 1995

Sarah and I had a wonderful morning together. We woke up around six o'clock, and she crawled into my hospital bed where we *snuggled* until breakfast. We talked about our house plans for more than two hours and got to spend some much-needed quiet time alone. For a while, we talked about the possibilities of the future. Later in the morning, it was back to reality. I am still too weak to shower or bathe myself, so Sarah had to do it for me. I doubt she ever thought her thirty-year old husband would be too weak to wash himself. I never did.

MONDAY, AUGUST 7, 1995

Sarah left today and Mom returned. It is the beginning of yet another long week ahead of me at UKMC. Kanga said all the tests seem to be normal. A couple of medication levels will be increased but nothing drastic. I slept a lot of the afternoon. My energy level is still not close to where it should be. Lois checked my PFT's [Pulmonary Function Test] today and they hit a record low, but it doesn't surprise me. Kanga said we still have about two weeks to go. I just have to be patient, something I am getting good at doing.

TUESDAY, AUGUST 8, 1995

I took sleeping medicine last night and spent most of today sleeping. I finally got some much-needed rest. I am still having breathing problems when I get out of bed and move around, but I am feeling better. I am still amazed at how weak I am. Today, I fell because of water on the floor. I am so weak that I could not stand back up, so I crawled to the bed and pulled myself up. This simple action wore me out. It is strange how your focus on things changes when you are on an organ waiting list. I, along with my family and friends, have become more aware of morbid things like accidents, murders, and other deaths. I heard on television tonight that the next two weeks are traditionally the deadliest on Kentucky highways because of people traveling before school begins in the fall. It is hard wanting new lungs as soon as possible, because that means someone has to die. That is hard to accept.

WEDNESDAY, AUGUST 9, 1995

It was a very quiet day in the hospital. I took more sleeping medicine last night and slept most of the morning. I did have some trouble during the night. I lost my balance when I went to the bathroom and could not get back to bed. I had to call the nurse and Mom for help. I can check off another low point in my continuing series of low points. Tandy came by and we discussed his lung transplant. He has been back in for four weeks with various rejections and infections and his breathing seems short and labored. He says he can tell a big difference in his breathing since the operation. I hope after my transplant, my breathing improves more. I just want my life to return to normal, and soon.

THURSDAY, AUGUST 10, 1995

The old Gospel hymn says "One day at a time, Sweet Jesus. That's all I'm asking from you." I seem to be in that mode on a daily basis, one more day of strength, wisdom, patience, and understanding about what is happening and is about to happen to me. There are no new developments in the hospital today. In the afternoon Mom's pastor, Chuck Pruitt, came to visit. It is good to have such a caring minister to visit with. He is the only person that has been there for me spiritually over the last few trying weeks. He is a good, caring, and sincere man. This has been the one time in my life when I needed spiritual guidance the most. My procedure is a very serious one, and there is a chance that I will not survive. I do not think anything will go wrong, but it would have been nice to have someone to talk it over with.

FRIDAY, AUGUST 11, 1995

It was two weeks ago that I came to the hospital, and it has been eight weeks since I left work for the last time. It is amazing how fast and how many things can change. Eight weeks ago, I left work at University Relations and two days later, I was admitted to UK, put on oxygen, and two days after that admitted to Intensive Care. Since then, I have not walked more than a few feet at a time, am on constant oxygen, and have been placed on a national organ donor donation list. Wow! What a busy eight weeks. Today, I did walk to the end of the hallway, a major accomplishment. It may not seem like much, but it means a lot to me. It is a step in the right direction. My PFT's were still very low today, and my oxygen saturation levels fell into the eighties after being off my oxygen for just a few minutes. Kanga said the Morphine ends early next week. I must work hard this weekend to wean myself off the drug. It is sometimes the only relief I can get for my breathing, and that concerns me. I am afraid that I have become dependent upon the drug to ease my breathing problems, a quick fix to an old problem. I lost another IV tonight. That makes six IV's since I was admitted. I only used four during the last hospitalization. It appears that my veins are getting tired and the medicines are beginning to get to them.

SATURDAY, AUGUST 12, 1995

It is another lost summer weekend at the University of Kentucky hospital. It was mostly a quiet day. I only had a few calls. I walked to the end of the hallway again tonight, another major milestone. I remember as a kid in the hospital, walking past someone in the hall that was learning to walk again, as I am now, and never giving it a second thought. They were always in my way and were walking too slow. I would simply walk around them, grumble something about being slow, and then speed on my way, barely glancing at the cause of the distraction before continuing with my life, until now. Now, other people walk quickly around me, because I am the distraction. I am that slow moving person learning to walk again with tubes hanging from my body. They are the ones in a hurry with places to go and people to see. That is not my case. I only have to walk, nowhere, anywhere. Just walk, and walk, and walk. Build up strength. That is what I continue to do ... walk, because I have nowhere to go ... for now.

SUNDAY, AUGUST 13, 1995

Today, I finally realized the significance of this summer. I have lost the summer of 1995. I have lost the first summer of my marriage. It is gone forever. The whole summer and all of its plans, gone! I had a poor night. My chest pains returned, and the nurse had to call the doctor for extra Morphine. I spent a restless night and did not sleep well. I had a good morning and was able to clean up. I can tell a difference in the amount I can do at once. I can see improvement ever so slowly. I just hope the lungs come soon. It was eight weeks ago today when I was first hospitalized. It has been a long and very trying eight weeks. My body and mind are tired. Something needs to give.

TOP 50 THINGS I MISSED DUR-ING THE SUMMER OF 1995:

50. Running through the newly cut, cool, crisp, dark green grass after it has just been mowed.

49. Running anywhere, or nowhere, on my own.

48. Kicking back in a country swing on a warm Sunday afternoon while nursing a frosty glass of lemonade that still has the seeds and pulp in the glass.

47. Driving down an unpaved country road that is so dusty, the world behind you, not to mention your friend and his car, disappears into a sea of swirling brown.

46. Eating a hot dog at Wrigley Field that's been cooking longer than it takes to get from Scottsville to Bowling Green on 231 when you are in a hurry.

45. Laboring to see a deer before the sun begins to melt behind the rolling hills at my grandparent's Kentucky farm.

44. Sipping a warm cup of coffee during a frosty, cool morning camping trip while watching the lightly colored, charcoal coffee steam swirl round and round as the light morning breeze gently whips the steam so the air can also enjoy the aroma.

43. Driving down a two-lane road while trying to avoid hitting an opossum that is standing in the center of the yellow lane while trying to become the first opossum in history to make it across the road without being turned into a pancake.

LaRecea Gibbs

42. The feeling you get when the pastor walks up to you at Bible School and asks if you will carry the American flag for the opening service.

41. That same feeling twenty years later when the pastor asks you to pray the benediction prayer on the spur of the moment after you just put a piece of gum in your mouth.

40. Sitting on the back porch listening to the cricket's play their medley of musical magic while watching the feisty fireflies flash feverishly to the rhythm of the insect's instrumental interludes.

39. Counting the countless stars in the sky and realizing that our problems are insignificant.

38. Eating tomatoes picked directly from the vine and smothered in salt.

37. The sucking sounds of carp and catfish feeding off bugs and lake grass as the dimming sunlight bounces off the ripples caused by their quest to get a meal.

36. The sound rain makes as it hits an old tin roof forming a symphony of showers that can never be matched nor forgotten, because God is the conductor.

35. Sitting with my feet dangling in the creek while tiny minnows nibble at my toes.

34. Slow Sunday mornings before church.

33. The Crayola rainbow of colors that God uses to paint the sunsets that seem to last forever, and we take for granted by barely looking upward.

32. Homemade ice cream.

31. Saturday morning coffee and cherry Pop Tarts while watching "The Bugs Bunny Show."

30. Cleaning out the garage and finding things you never knew you needed, forgot you had purchased in the first place, and are not sure how you have been living these last few months without them.

29. Five words: sweet corn on the cob.

28. Sitting on the riverbank watching my bobber rock side to side while a trophy bass tests the authenticity of my cricket and worm combination sandwich.

27. Eating outdoors.

26. Smelling flowers and never realizing it.

25. Driving down the highway and watching two baby calves run, jump, and kick for the first time in their new lives.

24. Driving by a field of newly cut hay.

23. Watching two birds fight over a piece of dropped hamburger bun.

22. Passing near a pond on a clear, breezy night and seeing the rippling reflections of the powder- white full moon dancing across the dark, warm water like diamonds sitting in a jewelry store window.

21. Stopping by a field and picking buttercups.

20. The smell of honeysuckles.

19. (Unable to read)

18. Barbecuing with friends on a Sunday afternoon.

17. The way the world smells when the sun shines following a late afternoon thunderstorm.

16. Ice cream that is melting so quickly that you cannot possibly eat it before it dribbles down your shirt.

15. A picnic.

14. Listening to the roar and crackle of a campfire.

13. Watching the morning river fog snake its way through the rocky and rolling Kentucky countryside.

12. Flying a Frisbee.

11. The smell of freshly laid blacktop along the highway and the sound those little stones make as they bounce upward and hit the underpinning of the car.

10. Walking barefoot through a freshly mowed yard while watching your feet turn Kermit the Frog green.

9. Sitting on a porch swing with someone you love.

8. Stopping in the middle of the road to pick up a turtle making sure it does not end up like the opossum when it tries to cross the road.

7. Taking a knife and saltshaker to the garden and eating a watermelon while sitting in the middle of the patch.

6. Watching a distant lightning storm illuminate the coal black, starless sky like a giant camera flash; taking pictures of our world from heaven.

5. Cotton candy and candied apples at the county fair.

4. Jumping in an old creek on a hazy, hot, and humid afternoon.

3. Sitting on the back deck while drinking a cup of coffee and reading the Sunday morning paper.

2. A magically sultry, summer sunrise snuggled around a time of day when only few are awake to appreciate its glory while the other half does not even bother to notice.

1. Number one memory about the lost summer of 1995:

Associated Press URGENT-URGENT-URGENT
[Lexington, KY] A 30-year-old Scottsville man's lifelong battle against cystic fibrosis ended today when doctors removed the scared lungs and replaced them with healthy lungs. Gibbs said, "With my new lungs and my new lease on life, my wonderful wife and supportive family and friends ... I would say the summer of 1995 is the summer we all found a lot about ourselves, our family and friends, about the kindness of a small community and the power of God through prayer. It will definitely be a summer to remember."

SUMMER OF 1995

Proposed [Actual]

Fishing at lake and pond [limited to early in spring]

Walk Long Creek, fishing [cancelled/unable to walk distance]

Set up deer stand [unable to accomplish]

Canoe with Hurt [unable, not enough energy]

Take Sarah to Opryland [unable]

Take Sarah to a Smokies weekend [unable]

Golf outings [unsuccessful attempt to play]

MC Allen Co. Junior Miss [hospitalized, cancelled]

MC Barren Co. Junior Miss [cancelled]

Judge Louisville Junior Miss [cancelled]

Weekend at cabin [postponed]

Weekend in Lexington [cancelled]

Nashville night out [postponed]

MONDAY, AUGUST 14, 1995

It was another painful night with little sleep. The doctors increased the morphine for one dose, but it did not help, because my IV went bad and most of the dose leaked out of the vein. My veins are not holding up well this time. For the first time ever, my veins are only lasting three or four days. It makes me wonder just how tired my body has become. X-rays showed infection in both lungs. Kanga said my body has become dependent on the Morphine that was ordered to ease the chest pain. He said over the next week or two, the Morphine levels will be lowered, so the body can adjust. The Morphine does its job well. Over the past few months, breathing has become a constant struggle. Sometimes each breath is a one-on-one basis. With the

LaRecea Gibbs

Morphine, my lungs relax, and for an hour or two, I can forget about chest pains and trying to breathe. Even though I am dependent, I would do it again. It was worth a few hours of easy breathing while I wait for this transplant.

TUESDAY, AUGUST 15, 1995

Today was another painful day. My chest pains are worse today since the Morphine has been decreased. The pain is constant and the lower doses of Morphine do not take it away. It only lessens it. I was able to take a shower today on my own. It felt good to be able to do that. It was difficult, but I made it through the shower. I can tell there is improvement. I walked to the end of the hall today without my oxygen. It was the greatest distance without O's that I have walked in eight weeks, and it showed. My oxygen level fell to fifty-four percent. It quickly rebounded to ninety-four percent, but I did not think it would drop that long in just two minutes of walking. I received thirty-six get-well cards today, which is a record. It took forty-five minutes to open and read all of the cards and letters. It was nice knowing that so many people are thinking of me during this difficult time. It has gotten to the point that I do not actually think of the transplant happening. The first week, I was ready for the call. If it came today or tomorrow, it would catch me by surprise. I have to get the expectation back and be ready.

WEDNESDAY, AUGUST 16, 1995

Today was a very eventful day. I met with the medical team concerning the Morphine situation. I have been on some type of Morphine, IV or oral, for two months. It is time to wean me off the drug or it could affect the transplant. All IV Morphine has been stopped today, and a new non-addictive painkiller has been started. It seems to be working well. It enabled me to get some much-needed rest today. Still no word of a transplant. Everyone is getting impatient. The transplant team, including Dr. Sakela, [transplant surgeon] visited me today and talked about how long it has been since they did a transplant. The last one was four weeks ago. Sabrina says it is time for another one, and I told her I was ready to be that one. Dr. Sakela says Dr. Kanga met him in the hallway and talked about my transplant. Sakela says whenever Kanga does that, a transplant usually happens within a week. That would be fine with me. Let's get this show on the road. I am ready to get on with my life. I am tired of it being on hold.

THURSDAY, AUGUST 17, 1995

I have had more breathing problems today and more chest pains. Walking is more difficult, and it seems I lost ground today. I got a call from WKU president, Dr. Thomas Meredith. It was a very warm, comforting phone call, and I enjoyed hearing from him very much. I typed an editorial about organ donations and sent copies to the *Herald Leader, Courier Journal, Park City Daily News, Citizen Times, and College Heights Herald.* All IV Morphine has been stopped and Phenergan has taken its place. It will help relax me, and it is non-addictive. It does make me sleepy, so if I take very much, I will be sleeping a lot.

FRIDAY, AUGUST 18, 1995

Nine weeks ago today, I walked out of my office at Western and had no idea that it was my last day for "only God knows" how long. I had a very shaky day today. It was probably due to the Morphine being cut. I slept most of the day today. I had much more trouble breathing last night, almost to the same extent as when I was admitted. Some of the problems can be attributed to the Morphine, both physical and emotional. Hopefully, it was a productive day in terms of the rest I was able to get. Other than that, it was a very slow day. I received eighteen get-well cards today. Roddy and Melissa came by and the two women went out to look at wallpaper. They bought me a shirt that reads, "My Lungs May Belong to UK but My Heart Belongs to Western."

SATURDAY, AUGUST 19, 1995

I got off to a slow, drowsy start today. Dr. Kanga came by early and seemed pleased with the way I am coming off the Morphine, but he still has some concerns. He wants me to stay alone some next week, so I will do more things on my own and become less dependent on others. Mom will stay home until Tuesday.

SUNDAY, AUGUST 20, 1995

It has been nine weeks ago today that this long journey began. That is when I was admitted to the U of K Medical Center beginning the longest nine-week struggle of my life. I never thought my life could change so quickly and so dramatically.

MONDAY, AUGUST 21, 1995

Seven weeks ago today, I was added to the organ donor list. School started back at WKU today without me. What's the saying, "Life Goes On"? Well, it sure is. I was not a part of the beginning as I should have been. I know where I am as the school year begins, but I wonder where I will be when the school year ends. I got up early with Sarah, so she could go back to work this morning. It is always hard to say goodbye, because anything can change at any time during the day. I did not get much sleep last night, less than two hours all together. Today, I got some sleep after doctors gave me some medication. Kanga and I are having some minor differences this hospitalization. He is just concerned and feels helpless while I am frustrated and feel helpless. We both have the faith and commitment in the other's opinion, but we have never faced such a serious situation together. We will win. Spent the day alone and really enjoyed it. This was the first time in nine weeks that someone was not watching me. Even though I needed someone to be here over the past weeks, it felt good today to have some independence. I got some rest in the afternoon, but the medicine they prescribed for me in an effort to make me sleep made me very confused. I received twenty-six get-well cards today. It is good to see how many people care for me during this difficult time.

TUESDAY, AUGUST 22, 1995

Today is the first day I have stayed alone in nine weeks. If you call being alone with 5,376 staff, patients, and employees being alone. I took things slowly and held up fair, but the more I did the more I wanted to do. This is known as "The LaRecea Gibbs Syndrome," a case study I am better understanding more and more each day. It has also helped me become more aware and sympathetic to what my father went through with his alcoholism. Though their cases were much more severe than mine were, the effects were not. I had my small taste of a lifestyle taken away in an instant as Mom's has been. I know what it feels like to want a drug to ease the pain, even if it means for only a few hours. The only difference is that my problem occurred during a hospitalization while I was under a doctor's care. I was not abusing the drug, just in need of it. That does not make it any easier physically or mentally, but it is working sometimes. I called Sarah, told her that I was shopping at Curly's in Cave City, [KY] and I would be home in about forty-five minutes. I then carried on a conversation with another person in my empty room while I continued to talk with Sarah. I did the same with Hurt when he visited. I would go to sleep and then wake up talking about something I was thinking about. I know Hurt thought I was out of my mind and he is probably right. I received twenty-three more get-well cards today, and we are beginning to run out of wall space to hang them. I am very, very tired and disoriented this afternoon and evening. Hurt came by as I was getting ready to take a nap, and I was talking off the top of my head. Sarah later called, and I did the same with her. She started crying. I explained that I had only spent a few hours the past two days sleeping. I am afraid she thinks it has: a) something to do with the Morphine; b) depression has turned me into a babbling idiot or c) her husband is an idiot and it took eight months for her to figure it out. It could be all of the above; nevertheless, for now, Sarah is at our home in Scottsville. I am in our summerhouse in Lexington. I got up early but did not sleep much last night and none during the day. Even though there was not a great number of visitors, the phone calls were numerous. There were a large number of medical students that started new shifts. One team that has started talking with me is the psychological team. I think it is a good idea and suggested it to Kanga in the first place. I need to know if these feelings, fears, and emotions that I am having are something everyone faces. I need to know how you deal with the fact that at anytime you could head for the operating room for a massive life-changing operation that could go wrong. Brother Pruitt is going to visit me tomorrow. Maybe we can have an inspirational conversation that I have needed but no one has done. Everyone else seems too busy.

WEDNESDAY, AUGUST 23, 1995

I had a very difficult night with very little sleep. I am also having a very difficult morning, and I am still having hallucinations such as being places where I am not. I am beginning to wonder if any more good days are coming. Mom is back today, and I am looking forward to her visit. I am having more and more trouble breathing. I slept off and on during the afternoon and had a fairly good evening, but then around seven, things started changing more rapidly. Oxygen levels dipped into the fifty percent range with little, if any, effort. I am growing more and more concerned about the disease's progress. I am on so many different drugs and medications that I am not always myself. My thinking is sometimes cloudy and confused.

THURSDAY, AUGUST 24, 1995

I had a very rough night that led to a very critical morning. Oxygen saturations fell and blood gases showed high levels of carbon dioxide. Kanga and Anstead talked about ICU again today, and there was more talk about the respirator. They want to give my lungs a few days to relax. I do not remember much over the past couple of days, so I am not able to make proper decisions. As the day progressed, my health returned and the move was postponed. Brother Pruitt was there for me again today. He visited for several hours and was very comforting at a much needed time. The doctors are adjusting my medications and I am beginning to tell a change. The transplant article appeared in *The Citizen Times* this week. My hands and legs are beginning to shake badly. Small tremors began a couple of days ago and have been increasing. I think the shakes are a combination of the Morphine, weakness, and large number of drugs. I hope it is a temporary thing.

FRIDAY, AUGUST 25, 1995

I slept most of the day because of medications. I am very groggy, and it has been a very difficult day, maybe the most emotionally straining day of my life. I asked Kanga if I was dying, and he said, "Yes." It was overwhelming to hear him say it. Later in the day, I asked Anstead the same question, and he agreed with Kanga. To hear your doctors tell you that you are dying is a feeling I cannot describe. I cried. I knew to be placed on a donor list meant your condition was terminal, but these guys seem to be talking months or weeks. For the first time in my life, I am afraid. I am not ready to die. I am a Christian, and I know Heaven awaits me, but I have too much left to do. I am too young. I decided not to listen to my doctors. I never had before so why start now?

SATURDAY, AUGUST 26, 1995

According to Dr. Anstead, I could be here until the transplant is completed. That could be days, weeks, or months. That will be fine if I can keep up my health in the hospital. I got sick in the afternoon and started vomiting. Doctors ordered a drug that knocked me out. I noticed again today that I am becoming more emotional and moody. I need to ask the doctors if my antidepressants were changed.

SUNDAY, AUGUST 27, 1995

Today is probably the quietest Sunday I have spent in the hospital. I had few visitors and few phone calls today. Hope, Donnie, Angela, and Julie came up in the afternoon, and Mom came back tonight. My breathing is getting worse again, and my depression seems to be coming back. They may have changed or stopped some of the drugs that affect my moods. I need to check on this. The article I wrote about transplants was printed in *The Park City Daily News* today. Maybe someone will be touched. Maybe it will cause someone to think. Maybe it will give someone a second chance at life ... or maybe a first chance. Maybe it can make a difference.

NEWSPAPER ARTICLE

Organ Donation: A Matter of Life and Unselfish Love

BY TODD GIBBS

What if your doctor said that because of the accelerated rate of your fatal disease, you have between six months to a year to live?

However, he gives you hope. There is a life-saving operation available that will replace your old, tired, diseased, damaged lungs with new healthy ones, enabling you to breathe normally for the first time in your thirty-year-old life. The only catch is that your new chance at life depends upon someone else's tragic death.

I'm a cystic fibrosis patient currently hospitalized at the University of Kentucky Medical Center. July 3, after thirty years of fighting lung infections, doctors placed my name on the national organ list for a double-lung transplant. Since then, my world has changed forever.

Up to this point, I have been very fortunate to live a fast-paced, active lifestyle. I am a council member for the city of Scottsville, a high school basketball referee, Sunday school teacher, and a deacon at Scottsville Baptist Church, and last December I married Sarah Smith of Western's public radio service. Life was good, and then everything changed overnight.

My health had been declining since some medication problems last summer, but the situation became worse over the past few months at an alarming and accelerated rate.

When I left work at WKU on June 16, I never dreamed how dramatically and quickly my life would change over the next few days. Two days later, I was hospitalized, placed on oxygen twenty-four hours a day, and confined to complete bed rest. It became worse, because two days later, I was in Intensive Care for the first time in my life, and doctors were preparing paperwork to add my name with those waiting for human organ donations.

Without the transplant, the cystic fibrosis will finally accomplish its one and only goal...to destroy its host. In this case, the host is me. With the transplant, the disease can never again cause me to breathe with difficulty, and the host will win. The choice was simple. I chose the transplant, because I like the host!

Now comes the most difficult part—waiting! The average wait for lungs in Kentucky is about three months. However, one never knows when the operation is going to occur. It could be within the next hour, tonight, tomorrow, next week, next month, or months from now. Once the lungs are found, I have three hours to get from Scottsville to Lexington for the eight-hour, life-changing, life-saving operation.

It is difficult to realize that while the procedure may allow me to live, it also means someone else must die. That is why organ donation is so special. It is the gift of life that is given at a time the donor's family is facing their lowest moment in life, the death of a loved one. It is a tragedy they turn into a triumph by giving life to one or more complete strangers. In fact, between eyes, heart, lungs, liver, skin, pancreas, arteries, veins, and bone marrow, one donor can change the lives of many people, including the recipient's family and friends. That is why donors and their families are true heroes.

Meanwhile, my wait continues, along with some fears. What if no one donates? What if my disease progresses too far before donor lungs are found? How long do I have to wait and put my life on hold? What if the new lungs do not work? What if the body rejects the new lungs? What if…?

At the same time, there are thousands of transplant hopefuls going through the same wait that I am, asking the same questions. Even though we may be waiting for different organs to save our lives, we are all waiting for one thing in common, the unselfish love from someone we will never meet, but who will be with us for the rest of our lives. We will also owe them for the rest of our lives.

Many of us are betting on that unselfish love. In fact, we are betting our lives on it.

There are more people needing organs than there are organs being donated. Each day organs that could have been donated are wasted, because families did not know about the donor's wishes or the need for life-saving organs, resulting in a lost chance at extending a life. That is unfortunate, because it means some person, who could have lived may die, waiting needlessly. You can be the difference! The lives you save could be someone you will never know or someone you have loved forever.

Call the Kentucky Organ Donors' Affiliates at 1–800–525–3456 or contact www.*kyorgandonor*.org or the national association at *www.donatelife.net*. Many people are waiting for your call. As just one of them, I thank you.

JOURNAL ENTRIES: AUGUST 28, TO SEPTEMBER 25, 1995

MONDAY, AUGUST 28, 1995

It has been two months or eight weeks or fifty-six days or 1,334 hours or 88,640 minutes or 4,838,400 seconds. That is how long it has been since I was added to the transplant list; much longer than I ever thought it would be. Today was an emotional day. Sarah went back to work, and that always makes me sad. I am on so many medications my thoughts are cloudy and confused. Kanga says they are not sure which medicines makes me shake, which medicines make me confused, which medicines are working, and which ones are not. It appears that we do not know much about anything we are doing. I had several anxiety attacks today, more than usual. I will ask Kanga if it has anything to do with reducing or changing medicines. Meanwhile, the tremors and shakes are getting worse. Mom massages my arms and legs, and it sometimes helps. At times, my legs are shaking bad enough it causes the bed to shake. My hands are shaking to the point that it is affecting my writing and the ability to feed myself. My left hand is the worst, but my right hand is bad also. My transplant article appeared in the *Louisville Courier Journal* today.

TUESDAY, AUGUST 29, 1995

TODD GIBBS HIGHLIGHTS FOR THE DAY

10. Woke up without a massive chest pain, even though oxygen tubing was wrapped around my neck causing my oxygen saturations to drop, my chest to ache, and the low oxygen alarms to sound. Good morning.

9. Morning medication time, which today consisted of seventeen different pills, one shot, two IV solutions, and two medicated breathing treatments. All of this happened before nine.

8. Took a sink bath that took forty-five minutes to accomplish, something that once took me ten to fifteen minutes. Just brushing my teeth without stopping for a breathing spasm is celebrated as a victory.

7. Kanga and I talked about stopping the IV drugs and going with a new round of oral antibiotics. The big drugs have run their course and it is time for something else. I hope plan three works better than the first two plans.

6. Walked to the end of the hall and pushed my own oxygen. Had to rest before I made the return trip. Tomorrow, I will try to make the trip twice a day, then add a day, and distance to each day thereafter.

5. Stayed more out of bed than in bed today.

4. Talked to God. A lot. I hope he is listening.

3. I cried, but I did not laugh. I cannot remember the last time I laughed. That is what I miss doing the most. Laughing. It is just nothing seems funny anymore. The world is a serious place all of a sudden. But I have always been able to laugh … until now. I miss laughing and smiling.

2. Wondering where my new lungs are and when will I get them, if I will get them.

1. [The last item on this list I was unable to read]

WEDNESDAY, AUGUST 30, 1995

Today was a good day. I spent the day out of bed walking and stirring around the room. My shakes and tremors are still very bad. My legs are shaking bad enough to wake me up at night. My handwriting is unreadable. I walked more today than I have since I was hospitalized ten weeks ago. It was difficult, but it felt great to get out of the room and walk on my own. Donnie may give Mom a break by coming to stay with me tomorrow. It would do well for the two of us to spend time together. We need to plan the tournament. I am not sure how much I will be with this year's LIS [Lady Invitational of the South] or where I will be. No matter what happens to me, I want the tournament to continue. I need that assurance from Donnie. I know he will give it to me. I have gotten many positive comments about my article that appeared in the papers. I found out it caused one lady to donate her daughter's heart to a heart patient. I may have helped save a life. That is a great feeling that I want to do repeatedly. That is what I need to do after I get my transplant, teach others about transplants and Jesus's love for them. That way I could give them life, twice!

THURSDAY, AUGUST 31, 1995

Goodbye August, hello September. I thought I would get my transplant in August. August, 1995, will go down as the most difficult August of my life, and I hope it goes down as the most difficult month of my life. September is *please* going to be the month for a transplant. I had a good day today. I walked downstairs and farther than I have walked in two months. I even walked down a flight of stairs in an effort to keep my legs working in all directions. Mom went home, and Donnie is staying with me tonight. He is a special friend, and I am glad he is here. I can tell that I am getting better and my outlook is more optimistic. Labor Day weekend is coming up. Transplants increase during the holidays. It is hard to believe that I was also in the hospital during the last big summer holiday weekend, the Fourth of July. I have placed copies of my transplant article on my door. People have been reading them and making copies of them all day. One lady told me a friend's daughter committed suicide and had always wanted her organs donated. The mother did what her daughter wanted, but she did not feel good about donating the organs. After receiving a copy of my article, the mother told her friend that her mind was at ease, and she feels like the story was written just for her. I am glad I helped her in some small way. I hope this is one step in many to come.

FRIDAY, SEPTEMBER 1, 1995

Here we go; a new month, a new weekend, a new holiday weekend, and a new babysitter, my third in as many days. I enjoyed spending time with Don yesterday, last night, and today. He is a truly special friend that I know I can always count on. He is more like my brother, always looking out for me.

SATURDAY, SEPTEMBER 2, 1995

It was a good day with a lot of good company and friends. I walked again today and stayed out of bed most of the day. I think I still look like a skeleton. The shakes are getting worse. I had another stomachache and vomited. They gave me some medicine to ease the cramps and it made me drowsy. After I woke up from my nap, Dad and Granny were here. Goforth [Minister of Youth and Music at Todd's church] stopped by tonight, and it was good to talk with him about spiritual matters. He can make you feel so comfortable. He is truly a gift of God to the Scottsville Baptist Church. I owe Goforth so much. He took me and has molded my spirituality. The holiday weekend is underway. I am nervous for the first time, because I know there is an increased chance the transplant could happen at any moment. Even though I am ready, I am nervous. I knew it would happen when I got comfortable and least expected it. I just feel like it is going to happen soon … real soon.

SUNDAY, SEPTEMBER 3, 1995

This all started eleven weeks ago today with the first hospitalization. Sundays at hospitals are so quiet. I woke up early and stared at the ceiling pondering important matters. Who will take care of Sarah if something happens to me? Have I accomplished what I should have up to this point in life? If the coyote catches the Road Runner and Sylvester catches Tweety, wouldn't their shows be cancelled? Questions, especially the last one, only God knows. I had many visitors today and held up well. I am still very groggy during the day, and I think it could still be side effects from some of the medicines. It is easy to lose track of days in the hospital. When I went to church every Sunday, it set my body's calendar for the week. Since I have not been to church in more than eleven weeks, the days and nights run together. I miss church. I have never gone this long without attending, and with God's help, I will never go this long again.

MONDAY, SEPTEMBER 4, 1995

It is another holiday in the hospital. I spent my thirtieth birthday, Easter, July 4, and now Labor Day, hospitalized. Hopefully, I will have my new lungs before the next holiday, which would be Halloween! I had lots of company today, and I had a good day. I am still very tired and had to take several naps in order to make it through the day. The holiday weekend is over and still no lungs, but I am getting stronger and stronger each day. I am able to walk more and some of my upper body muscle strength is returning. I am still shaking so bad that writing and feeding myself are challenges at times. As I get more and more exercise, I am gaining more self-control. Angela just called. She said she just knew today would be the day, and she refused to leave the house all day waiting for the call. I think that CF has been as hard on Angela and Hope as it has me. I hope they realize how much I appreciate and love them for always being there. I think we're closer than most siblings are, and that's probably a result of my CF. It's just another positive aspect of CF that I need to remember. I think everyone expected something this weekend. I know it will happen when we least expect it. I keep telling them we are dealing with God's plan and not ours. If there is one lesson God is teaching a lot of people, it is patience.

TUESDAY, SEPTEMBER 5, 1995

"Good things come to those who wait." I keep saying this over and over again. Todd Hurt visited today, and I was more alert this time. I did have some trouble when I tried to get ready to walk downstairs with him. I went into the bathroom to put on a pair of sweat pants and fell against the shower. When I tried to get up, the table slipped and I fell harder on the floor. It took Mom, Hurt, and a nurse to get me back to the bed. It was very embarrassing for my best friend to see me like this, but I think he understands.

WEDNESDAY, SEPTEMBER 6, 1995

Day number forty-one began well and then went downhill quickly. The first few hours I was up and very mobile. I met with Kanga and Lois, and he told me how proud he was with my improvement. He explained that I should expect slow progress because I was sicker than I may realize. Not long after Kanga left, my breathing started getting worse as my lungs tightened. My saturations dropped into the sixties and seventies, and I was confined to bed. I spent all of the afternoon very sick in bed and slept most of the time. Mom monitored the levels and alerted the nurses when the levels fell to critical levels. I had a very difficult night. I felt like this was a big step backwards.

THURSDAY, SEPTEMBER 7, 1995

After a very restless night, I woke up around six-thirty and read the paper. It has been another difficult day. I slept most of the day because oxygen levels were low, and energy and exercise levels were nonexistent. Mom continues to massage my arm and leg muscles in an effort to keep them from shaking. It seems to really help, especially my arm muscles that are sorer and sorer each day because of the increased exercised I am trying. Jeff Younglove [friend, coworker at Western and a reader at his wedding] came to visit today. It was the first time I had seen him since I left work more than two months ago. It was good to hear about office matters at Western. I miss it so much. I miss going to work. I miss the morning drive to Bowling Green with my wife. I miss our morning coffee together. I miss that look Sarah gives me when I suggest we are running late. I miss calling Sarah during the day to see how her day is going. I miss walking around campus and seeing old friends and places with special college memories. I miss getting in the car and driving to the lake, or the farm, or anywhere. I miss going to church and Sunday school. I miss everyday actions I used to take for granted. Now, I long to do them once again.

FRIDAY, SEPTEMBER 8, 1995

Friday, July 28 is the day I was admitted, forty-three days ago. I would have never believed it would have lasted this long. This has been the most difficult period of my life, and I know it is just getting started with the really difficult time still to go. I am getting very, very tired both mentally and physically. Each day I seem to get a little weaker, less determined and more pessimistic. I am so tired of waiting and tired of trying to be upbeat for everyone. I want the transplant so I can get on with my life!

SATURDAY, SEPTEMBER 9, 1995

Another weekend is here. The days are beginning to run together, and it is impossible to separate days or events. Days seem meaningless and unimportant and nights are even worse. I am not sure how much longer I can take it. I dream of the old times: doing what I wanted anytime I wanted; going for drives; going to movies; going out to eat; going to the farm; going to the grocery; going to work; going to church; just being normal. I wonder if those days will ever come again. Sometimes I think yes and sometimes I fear not. Time will tell.

SUNDAY, SEPTEMBER 10, 1995

No earthshaking events took place in UKMC room 619 on this date. Visitors came and left. Nurses came and left. Medications were taken and treatments were given. No tests or procedures were conducted. No major changes were noted. Twelve weeks ago today, I was admitted to UK for the first round and the start of this situation. Twelve long weeks. I am still amazed at the speed the disease progressed and how quickly my entire lifestyle changed. I have gone from being a respected member of the community, a deacon, city councilman, coordinator of radio and television services for a college university. All of that seems gone at this point. I wonder if I will ever get any part of it back. "A time for every purpose under the heavens…" I do not know the purpose of any of this. Maybe I am not supposed to know the purpose right now. Maybe that is part of God's plan.

MONDAY, SEPTEMBER 11, 1995

Another day in the hospital. I went outside in a wheelchair for the first time in forty-six days. It felt good to have the sunshine on my face and feel the cool breeze against my skin. I miss the simple things in life that we take for granted each day. The simple things we overlook.

TUESDAY, SEPTEMBER 12, 1995

Sarah got up early this morning to head back to WKU to work. As I watched her get ready to leave, I found myself longing to be able to do what she was doing, going to work. I just want to get back to normal. I sometimes think I will wake up and all of this will be a bad dream. I wish it was a bad dream. Each day takes a little more out of me, and I am not sure what to do to keep that from happening. I spend my days thinking about the past and the things I am missing. I am not thinking about the future, and I know that is not healthy. One of the greatest gifts God has given us is our ability to remember. It is like having your own personal VCR and VCR tape library in your own head. That is what helps me make it through the day, reflecting back over the good times I have had. I wonder if those days are gone forever or will I be able to add new volumes to the list? Time will tell.

WEDNESDAY, SEPTEMBER 13, 1995

I do not feel like I am making any productive progress. If anything, I feel I am close to the same level as when I was admitted forty-eight days ago. Each day I get more tired, and I am noticing that it is getting more difficult focusing or concentrating on things. I lose focus quickly or my mind wanders off the subject. I have trouble recalling conversations, information, discussions, etc. Kanga wants me to consider having an implantable venous access system in my arm. My veins are getting tired and becoming more and more difficult for the nurses to stick. Today, it took three tries before the nurse hit the vein. Since I have so many sticks ahead of me, Kanga thinks it would be the easy and best way to proceed. I guess I agree and will have the procedure done. It is another victory for CF, another loss for Todd. It seems like that has been the case a lot lately. That's one trend that must stop!

THURSDAY, SEPTEMBER 14, 1995

I had lots of visitors today: Donnie, Goforth, Dr. Price, [Todd's pastor] Muppet, and Cheryl Coots. Donnie and I worked on the LIS tournament today. It is hard to believe it is just a little over three months away. I now know my role in this year's tournament will be dramatically affected by the transplant. I wrote letters today to the coaches and media explaining my situation and how it will and will not affect the tournament. It is good to have someone like Donnie to help handle the tournament. It will go well. It has been another long day. I slept a large part of the day mainly because my breathing was poor today, and I did not get out of bed. I miss just being at home, sitting on the front porch, enjoying spending time with my wife and dog. I miss being at my house, sitting in my chair, watching my big screen television. It is not the big things I miss. It is the everyday common things I long to do, walking without breathing hard and riding to work with Sarah. I miss the simple things, things we take for granted every day. Maybe that is the most important lesson of the ordeal; never take anything for granted. Tonight while watching "ER" there was a wedding scene. It made me reflect back on the day Sarah and I were married. I have been thinking about how beautiful she was and how it was the most perfect and special day of my life. Looking back on times like that is helping me get through times like this. Each day gets harder and harder and makes me wonder if the lungs will ever come. I know, through my faith in God, that it is under control in his plan; but I am human, and I am trying to learn patience during the most stressful and trying time of my life.

FRIDAY, SEPTEMBER 15, 1995

Today is day fifty. Today, the local CBS affiliate, WKYT, interviewed Kanga and me about the "power of prayer" in the healing process. It is a special series that will run in November. They talked to us about our belief on the importance of prayer in the healing process. I would have never dreamed that I would have to wait so long before a transplant. I feel so tired. My body feels tired. I will not give up though. I will not give in. Brother Pruitt, Dad, and Granny all visited today. They were good visits and not all at once. Mom left with Brother Pruitt so she could follow him back in case she had more car trouble

SATURDAY, SEPTEMBER 16, 1995

A rainy day outside makes for a better day inside the hospital. Howard [Ives] visited today. It is good to see old friends like Howard, because it gives me a chance to reflect back to happier times of my life. Howard has always been a good friend, and we have shared some wonderfully funny times when life seemed a lot simpler. I long for those days again. Saturday spent with friends on the lake, or the farm, or at the house, or at the movies, or at a thousand other places far away from the halls of the UKMC. That is what I am working for again. That is what I will achieve.

SUNDAY, SEPTEMBER 17, 1995

Day fifty-two at the UKMC is a Sunday. Another Sunday without going to church. I wonder what it will feel like the next time I walk through the church doors. Angela, Hope, Uncle Glyndle, Aunt Nadine, Danny, Sherry, Beau [cousins] Uncle LC, Aunt Mildred, Greg, and Theresa [cousins] came to visit today. It was good to see my family. Theresa cut my hair and brought me cookies while Aunt Nadine gave me a fruit basket.

MONDAY, SEPTEMBER 18, 1995

My story ran in the *Herald* today. I had a woman from Food Services who brought me a balloon after reading the article. She had a family member who had an organ transplant and enjoyed the article. I found out during the morning rounds that Dr. Kanga's father was murdered in Pakistan. His father was dragged from his car and killed in the middle of the day. Kanga is going home to be with his mother for a couple of weeks. He leaves on Friday. I hope when he returns I'll have new lungs to greet him. Once again, terrorists have disrupted and destroyed the lives of faces they will never see.

TUESDAY, SEPTEMBER 19, 1995

I got to spend some time with Kanga and got to talk to him about his father. We gave him a plant, and he seemed very touched. Tomorrow the ABC affiliate, WTVQ, is going to interview me about organ transplants. I hope it goes well.

WEDNESDAY, SEPTEMBER 20, 1995

I woke up this morning with severe back problems. I could not walk or even stand under my own weight. The pain was intense, but is controllable with pain medication. Doctors are not sure what has caused the latest problem, but they are not overly concerned. Sky Lancey, the news anchor for Channel 36, did the interview today about organ transplants. The interview went well and everyone seemed happy with my answers. I was not overly impressed with the story they aired. While it was positive, it looked like it was compiled in a hurry. A woman from KODA was with the team and thanked me for the articles that appeared in the papers. She told me that each time a story appears in a paper, they get a rush from that newspaper's service area. I can make a difference. The KODA woman said they wanted to hurry and get my lungs so I could be a spokesperson for the group. That would be wonderful.

THURSDAY, SEPTEMBER 21, 1995

I started the day, day fifty-six, at four a.m. when I fell while trying to go to the bathroom. I had to yell for Mom, and she got the nurses to help put me back in my bed. It was a very traumatic experience. I have started working on trying to regain the strength I have lost over the past few days. I gain a little and then lose a little. It is a tough day-by-day battle, and there are no days off. It seems like June 18, the first admission date, was a lifetime ago. It seems like the last time I worked at Western was another lifetime. It seems like forever since I saw Barkley [Todd's dog] and my house. I saw Dr. Kanga tonight for the last time before his trip to Pakistan. He seemed sad and almost reflective as he said goodbye. They will be in my prayers during this stressful period in his life, and maybe when he comes back I can give him a special present, me with new lungs. WBKO used some of WTVQ's video footage last night and this morning. I am not sure how they found out that Bowling Green and Scottsville were so close together and WBKO might be interested. Maybe WBKO did the contacting. Who knows and who cares? They are doing lung transplants as I type. A heart patient and a liver patient are each getting an organ. No CF patients received any organs this time around. Whitney [another CF patient waiting for a transplant] is downstairs in need of type O, which this was, but the lungs were out of her weight range. Sabrina was still happy about the transplant saying these things run in cycles. She then said to get ready. I told her I had been ready for two months.

FRIDAY, SEPTEMBER 22, 1995

I had a rough night last night. Mom spent a lot of time with the nurses trying to take care of me. I went to the bathroom around two a.m. and on the way back, I lost all of my air. Oxygen levels fell to the sixties and once in the fifties. I had to take two extra treatments and got very little sleep. I am getting so tired of this. I just want to get better and get my new lungs. The problem is not knowing when it is going to happen or what will happen after the surgery.

SATURDAY, SEPTEMBER 23, 1995

Oh, what a night! Oxygen levels fell to record lows and for no apparent reason. At one point, levels went to the forties during a severe coughing spell. I am taking more respiratory treatments than any other time in my life. Everything they say do, I do. Everything they say try, I try.

SUNDAY, SEPTEMBER 24, 1995

The Holland Baptist Church brought two vans full of church members to visit today. Granny was among the group, so she helped. The visits went well, and it was very good to see all of them. During the night, I went to the bathroom and the oxygen tank I was using ran out. My oxygen levels sank and I panicked. The rest of the night was long and stressful with saturation levels dropping into the sixties.

MONDAY, SEPTEMBER 25, 1995

Today was a very difficult day. It started with a meeting of the minds between the medical staff, pharmacist, and me. We all agreed the medicine is working, and none of us can understand why my breathing and the oxygen levels are so low. I tried sleeping in the afternoon, but it did not work. That night was the worst of my life. At times, I wondered if I would make it.

Note: This was Todd's last journal entry—the last words he left behind. He died in the early morning hours of Friday, October 13, 1995. He was placed in ICU, on a respirator, three days earlier. Five days later, matching lungs became available.

PART II
TODD'S JOURNEY
THROUGH THE EYES
OF HIS MOTHER

Note: This section of the book tells Todd's story from the viewpoint of a mother who tries to achieve a somewhat normal family life in spite of having a child with a fatal illness. I hope it conveys the joy of that life as well as the difficult moments. The good times far outweighed the bad.

"HOW LONG DO I HAVE TO LIVE, MAMA?"

Obstacles: he went over them, around them, and sometimes even through them, in spite of cystic fibrosis. Cystic fibrosis killed him five days after his thirty-first birthday, but, oh, the living he did before CF won the war! His disease never became the focus of his life. It was just an obstacle that interrupted his life when he was hospitalized.

When Todd was seven, he asked if CF killed children. I knew that someday he would personalize the question of death and CF and ask if *he* was going to die. I had plenty of time to prepare an answer, but I had not done so. It was a routine clinic visit that turned into the moment I had long dreaded.

Todd, then eleven, had just learned about the death of a friend who also had cystic fibrosis. He was not only grieving the loss of a friend, but, also, suddenly facing his own mortality. Dry eyed, but suddenly far too mature for his young age, he looked at his doctor, then me. He asked, "How long do I have to live, Mama?"

It had begun as an ordinary day, as least as far as clinic visits were concerned. I was driving Todd to Lexington for his regular checkup. We left home in the early morning hours, so he was using the time to catch up on his sleep. The one hundred sixty mile drive had become a routine trip, and I drove without thinking, using the time to daydream and organize my thoughts. I seldom had time to do that at home. I was the wife of a farmer, the mother of two active girls, five and nine, and the caregiver for Todd and his medical needs. I was also a part-time college student. Time to think without interruption was something rare for me.

I enjoyed looking at the trees all dressed in their splendid colors that only fall can paint. I was grateful that we could enjoy another summer day before the frosty mornings of October brought winter. I was also grateful that this was a routine visit without the worry that Todd would be admitted for another long hospitalization. He had been doing better the past month, so I had put behind me, momentarily, both the fear with which I had lived since Todd's diagnosis and the realization that he had been loaned to us for just a few years.

Traffic on the interstate was light and when Todd awoke, I enjoyed his company. He shared with me his hopes and plans for the future. I could almost forget that the future looked terribly bleak for him. Now our ordinary visit had turned my world upside down.

I put my arms around Todd's thin shoulders and wished my stronger ones could carry his load. All I could do was share with him that terrible moment of heartbreak.

I was thankful for a wonderful, understanding doctor, Dr. David Wilson. Dr. Wilson had been his physician for six years and cared deeply for his patients' emotional health as well as their physical problems. He answered Todd's question by explaining, "Todd, I can't tell you how long you have to live. Only God knows that. I believe he wants us to live each day fully, doing something for him. Then if he calls us at seven or seventy, our life has had the meaning and fulfilled the purpose he intended."

He went on to explain that the average lifespan, at that time, was fourteen years for a child born with CF. Then he told of a patient age twenty-seven that had CF and was attending college. He spoke about the advances that research had brought in the last decade. He explained that twenty years before, a child born with cystic fibrosis rarely lived to reach school age. Now there were CF patients attending college, marrying, and assuming important places in society.

D.K., Todd's friend who had died, had been one of those. At age twenty-one, he was a basketball manager at his university and making big plans for his future. He and Todd had been roommates in the hospital only three months earlier, one of the firsts for D.K. Dr. Wilson and I thought it would be good for Todd to become friends with someone who looked perfectly healthy and was living a normal life. All the other CF patients whom Todd had met through his numerous hospitalizations were very ill. Several with whom Todd had become friends had died. Being with D.K. could show him that he might be able to accomplish some of his dreams.

Two and a half months after that first meeting, D.K. visited our home for the weekend so he and Todd could attend the wedding of a favorite nurse. They had become fast friends, in spite of the age difference. D.K. had inspired all of us because he seemed to be winning the war with this deadly disease. The next weekend, he played in a golf tournament, entered the hospital that week, and died shortly after. The young man whom we hoped would be an example that the CF battle might be won had lost his war.

Trying hard to choke back the tears for his friend, Todd said to his doctor, "If D.K. could die three months after his first hospitalization, as much as I've been in the hospital I could be dead in three months, couldn't I?" He already knew the answer himself.

The drive home was a difficult one, just my son and I trying to deal with one of the most difficult moments of our lives. After a long silence, silently praying that God would give me guidance to help my son with his pain, I placed my hand on his knee and asked, "What is it Todd?"

"Mom, I've been thinking. When I die, I want to donate my eyes, heart, and kidneys for transplants so they can help other children. Nobody would want my lungs." [Todd always injected a bit of humor in any serious situation.]

He had witnessed the miracle that donated organs had brought to other children while being hospitalized in the large teaching hospital, the A.B. Chandler Medical Center on the University of Kentucky campus. In fact, he met one of his closest friends, Roddy Parsons, when Roddy was hospitalized with kidney failure. He received his transplant and they remained close friends. Later, they would serve as groomsmen in each other's weddings.

I marveled that Todd was thinking of others when his hurt was so deep. Once again, I asked myself, "Oh, God, why Todd?"

Later, during the drive home, Todd said, "Mom, I've been thinking. If I die, I'd want Steve to be a pallbearer, but that little runt couldn't carry a casket." Steve Cornwell was a classmate and was small in stature like Todd.

Although weighing only fifty-seven pounds at age eleven, Todd displayed the wisdom of a much older soul. That Christmas, after visiting the family of a friend at the funeral home, Todd looked carefully at the many floral arrangements sent to express sympathy. Later he said, "Mama, flowers are just a waste of money when someone dies. They just wilt and then there is nothing. When I die, I want everyone to send money to the UK playroom. They really need some new toys. Maybe they could send their money to CF for research, and they would find a cure." There was no sadness in his voice, just an acceptance of what might happen.

On that lonely road, with the sun slowly fading and the signs of fall now reminding me of death, I promised Todd that I would see that his wishes were fulfilled. Finally, sleep brought peace to Todd. I continued the drive remembering the day this precious boy was loaned to us.

IN THE BEGINNING

Since a little girl, my dreams consisted of marrying that special man and becoming a mother. I also hoped to teach English someday in high school, but it was a poor third. My husband, Donald, and I began dating during our sophomore year of college. Although we came from the same county and attended the same rural high school, we had never dated. After a chance meeting on the university campus, we began dating. Very soon, we knew we wanted to share our lives.

Our August wedding, six months later, was a dream come true for me. Walking down the aisle in my flowing white dress, the church filled with friends and relatives wishing us a joyous life together, tears of joy rolled down my cheeks. We did not realize our genes carried the potential of heartbreak for our children.

After a week in the mountains, we returned home and rented a tiny apartment. I enjoyed decorating it and making it uniquely our own. Soon the summer was over and time to return to school. I commuted each day while Donald became a part-time student and full-time aide for the Soil Conversation district.

When I became pregnant five months later, I was ecstatic. I marveled at the changes in my body and thrilled at the first fluttering of life. Fear was not a part of this pregnancy. We had never heard of cystic fibrosis and, even if we had, there was not a test in '64 that could detect carriers.

Todd was born October 8, 1964. It was the most exciting moment I had ever experienced. I welcomed each pain of labor and thrilled at the marvel of nature as my body worked to produce a new life. I watched Todd's birth through a mirror the doctor had arranged. [A rare event for our small hospital] He looked perfectly healthy at birth. I thought no other baby was as beautiful as mine, no other mother as happy.

Donald and I moved to the farm, and I postponed my education to become a full-time mother and wife. I never questioned my fulfillment as a woman. I felt completely happy with my new life. I had what I had always dreamed.

Three weeks after Todd's birth, he became seriously ill. He was in critical condition for several days. Doctors could not decide what was wrong. He had projectile vomiting and lost three ounces in three days, an alarming amount for a baby weighing 6 lbs.13 ozs. at birth. Doctors said he had an intestinal blockage that might require surgery. Now, I realize that was a symptom of cystic fibrosis, [meconium ileus], but our pediatrician had never seen a CF patient before and did not recognize the symptom. Time seemed to stop as our tiny son fought for his life. I had no idea at the time that it was only the first fight in a thirty-one year war.

Finally, doctors decided he had a milk allergy. They changed his formula to soybean milk. He began to improve, but the vomiting continued. At six weeks, the doctor changed him to homogenized milk, and he began to gain weight rapidly.

Each day brought a rediscovering of the joys of life as I watched my son grow and develop his own personality. There was no indication that a deadly disease was developing in his body. At nine months, Todd won the baby contest at the local fair based upon the healthiest, prettiest baby with the most charming personality. It was around this time that problems began that we later learned were the beginning symptoms of cystic fibrosis.

Todd kept coughing, and every time he was x-rayed, doctors would say his lungs were full of infection. They diagnosed him with asthmatic bronchitis or allergic bronchitis. Nights became a torment for him as the coughing continued. I told the doctors he seemed to cough almost every breath until he gagged and vomited what looked to be just mucus. They must have thought I was just a new mother greatly execrating her baby's problems.

LaRecea Gibbs

Doctors were perplexed, because in most ways, he looked like a happy, healthy baby.

Twenty-eight months after Todd's birth, a baby girl joined our family. Now my dreams seemed complete, except for my desire to become a teacher. I chose the name Angela. To me she was truly a little angel sent from heaven. Todd adored his baby sister and he soon became her hero.

THE DIAGNOSIS OF CYSTIC FIBROSIS

We were still spending many sleepless nights because of Todd's coughing and frequent infections. Angela, also, had pneumonia several times. We tried all the advice of doctors and, in desperation, even tried home remedies of well-intentioned friends. Nothing seemed to help. Finally, our family doctor recommended a pediatric allergist in the nearest large city.

Donald and I were making big plans for the future, dreaming of the life we hoped to have since I would soon be teaching and adding another income. We hoped to buy a farm, build a house, and enjoy watching our children grow. We, also, hoped to add to our family after I became an established teacher. We did not realize our little world was about to explode in our faces.

The allergist was a big, gruff-looking man who was putty in the hands of a child. Todd immediately felt comfortable with him. After taking a case history and doing a physical exam, Dr. Bishop called us into his office. He told us that although he believed Todd did have allergies, he suspected there was something else wrong with his lungs. He wanted to do another test before beginning the allergy tests. It was a salt test used to diagnose a disease of which we had never heard, cystic fibrosis. Since the doctor did not want to alarm us needlessly, he did not explain how serious it was, and we were wonderfully ignorant.

It was the month before Todd turned six when he was diagnosed. CF is a genetic disease affecting the endocrine glands, especially the digestive system and lungs. It causes the mucous glands to produce thick, sticky, glue-like mucus in the lungs, which becomes an ideal breeding ground for bacteria. Frequent infections occur destroying the lungs and eventually robbing the person of the "breath of life," causing death.

When both parents carry the CF gene, there is a twenty-five percent chance the child will have CF, a fifty percent chance he will only be a carrier, and a twenty-five percent chance he will neither have the disease nor carry the gene. Doctors told us that Todd would not live beyond the age of twelve.

Thanks in large part to the efforts of the National Cystic Fibrosis Foundation, the average age for a person with CF is now thirty-eight years instead of the twelve years when Todd was diagnosed in September, 1970.

The salt test was positive. Then our nightmare began. Dr. Bishop told us a few facts about CF. Although it affects many glands in the body, the digestive system and lungs are the worse, especially the lungs where complications occur that usually cause death.

The ride home was a nightmare, but we clung to the hope that the test was wrong. Dr. Bishop gave us that hope by suggesting we repeat the test before making a definite diagnosis. We returned three days later and were elated when the test results came back negative. Two different labs had done the tests. He wanted us to return the next day to repeat the test. A lab at Vanderbilt University Hospital would conduct the test. We were so sure the first test had been incorrect that we celebrated by taking the children to the state fair in Tennessee before returning to our home in Kentucky.

We returned the next morning—test positive! Two to one and the score was not going in our favor. Dr. Bishop asked the lab to do one more test, just to be certain. They repeated the test that afternoon. The waiting was torture. I realized later that the kind-hearted doctor wanted to be positive before he diagnosed CF, because he knew much better than we what lay ahead. I think he wanted to remove any doubt in *his* mind.

As we waited for the results of the fourth test, we watched our son playing in the doctor's office. It seemed impossible that he could have a deadly disease. He did not look sick. He was so happy, with such a winning personality that all the nurses and staff kept talking about how special he was. It couldn't be serious, could it? Allergies? Yes, that made sense. Then Todd would start to cough, a cough so deep and hard all eyes were upon him. Other parents looked afraid as if their child was in danger of catching something terrible. The fear would come back. Could Todd really have cystic fibrosis, a disease that had been unknown to us a few days earlier; a disease we unknowingly carried in our genes that could kill our child before he had a chance to really live?

The waiting became almost unbearable, and I prayed silently, "Please, God, let Todd be okay, but if it is not your will, please give me strength. I don't think I can survive losing this child."

Finally, the results came. I knew immediately by the compassion in the doctor's eyes what he was going to say. The test was positive. Three positive sweat chloride tests, combined with Todd's history and physical exam, left no doubt as to the correct diagnosis. There was no time for tears. We had to face our son and had many things to learn about caring for him.

The news devastated our parents. All of us had placed so much hope on the negative test. Donald and I were lost in our grief. Our outward appearance was calm, but each of us was fighting a battle within ourselves. That night in bed, I turned to him in tears, but he was too hurt himself to comfort me. We lay so close, yet so far apart.

We read the books the doctor gave us and began to learn about the disease that would eventually become a big part of our lives. We learned that CF is the most common genetic disease and second only to cancer in diseases that kill children. The thick mucus in the lungs causes the horrible cough with which we had become so familiar. We also learned that a CF child often lacks an important enzyme necessary for digestion of food and, as a result, they are sometimes small and thin in spite of enormous appetites. One thing was especially significant. These children lose a lot of salt when they sweat, and therefore often have a salty taste. I remembered Todd's aunt kissing him as a baby and remarking, "I thought babies were supposed to be as sweet as sugar. You taste salty."

We knew we must try to maintain a life as normal as possible, so I returned to the university. Sometimes tears would fill my eyes in the middle of a lecture, and I would think about what I might lose, instead of what I had.

Since Angela also had frequent pneumonia, we decided to test her. Once again, I heard the news, "test positive." I hugged my little three year old, curly haired daughter and let the tears fall. How could I stand this? How could God be so unfair? All I ever wanted was to be a mother and just when my dreams seemed almost complete, they were being shattered before my eyes.

Again, a strength I had not known existed gave me the courage to dry my eyes. There was much to learn in order to take care of my children. Tears would have to wait.

We began learning how to do the postural drainage that both would need. The children were placed in several different positions, sometimes head down, while being pounded with a cupped hand to loosen the mucus in each lobe. We did this twice a day on each child for forty-five minutes. That meant Todd had to awaken for school much earlier than most children did, so we could do his therapy. [Now, most patients use an automatic vest.] I also learned to watch for potential lung infections.

The children had to sleep in a mist tent. The tent put a fine mist into their lungs to help loosen the mucus. It also soaked the bedding, so I had to change the beds daily. Every day, each tent had to be taken apart and carefully cleaned. I washed the tent portion in the bathtub, and then hung it outside to dry. The ultrasonic part was much more complicated to clean.

So much time was now required to care for my children that I knew, once again, I would have to postpone my dream of becoming a teacher. The next day I drove the forty miles to the university to withdraw. I was feeling sad as tears blurred my vision. I

LaRecea Gibbs

looked at my college ring and realized it would be a long time before I deserved to wear it. I prayed for courage to do what I knew I must and strength to enjoy my children while I still had them.

Before going to the registrar's office, I went to talk to my advisor, Dr. Woods, who was chair of the English Department. I had worked with him under the student work program. Actually, I was a little afraid of him and thought him to be gruff. That day, I saw a completely different side, one that was warm and caring.

He shared with me that he and his wife had always wanted children, but were not blessed with them. He spoke how he always wanted a little child to sit on his lap and watch him grow. He added, "They say it is better to have loved and lost than to never have loved at all. I believe it is better to have a child and lose it than to never have a child at all. My wife and I will not have those memories to warm our hearts when we are old, but you can. Now, you forget about college. Go home, start making those memories, and postpone your degree. Western will always be here for you. You'll have those memories to get you through when that is all you have." I have thought of his words many times.

ADJUSTING TO LIFE WITH CYSTIC FIBROSIS

Donald and I had hoped to have more children, but since CF is an inherited disease, we decided not to risk it. When I learned a month later that I was pregnant, we were both upset. Was it right to bring another child into the world when we knew it had a twenty-five percent chance of having to suffer and die? Was it fair to Todd and Angela when they needed so much care themselves? Could we care for another child when doctors warned us that our children might have to spend much time in hospitals and the medical expenses would be enormous?

During the next months, I existed on a seesaw of despair and hope. One day I would firmly believe that this child would also be born with CF. I would never have the chance to watch one of my children grow into adulthood. The next day, I would be convinced that this child was a special bonus from God, one to bring us joy when we no longer had Todd and Angela.

As my due date approached, I finally gained a peace. My mother kept saying, "LaRecea, just put it in God's hands. He'll never give you a cross to bear without giving you the strength you need to bear it."

Shortly after their diagnosis, Todd was watching the Jerry Lewis telethon for MS. Each Labor Day, the Holland Lion's Club sponsored a community fish fry at the Community Center across the road from our home. The men did all the cooking, except for the dessert. Wives of the members furnished that.

I was in the kitchen making my dessert. My due date for Hope's birth had come and gone. We had just learned that a friend's family had suffered a tragedy. A father and his son had been killed by lightening while loading tobacco into the barn. I was still dealing with the changes cystic fibrosis had brought to our lives and, overall, I was having a bad day.

Todd came to the kitchen asking if he could call the telethon to make a donation. He had saved a little money from gifts and doing chores and wanted to pledge it to MD. I suggested he wait and give his money to the upcoming CF campaign. Todd answered, "But, Mom, they are so much worse off than I am." We called the TV station so he could make his pledge.

Mother had surgery the day before my baby was born. She had cancer. I would lose my mother in a few months, but God had blessed us with a baby girl.

We named her Hope. That name seemed fitting because so many of our hopes depended upon her being free of CF. Six months later, tests showed she truly was our hope. She does not have CF.

We were always honest with the children about why they were sick so often. Since Angela had been doing great the past year, we decided to test her again. Her test was negative. She does not have CF. That night, she prayed, "Thank you Jesus I don't have CF. Thank you I don't have to sleep in that tent anymore. I'm so happy you made me well." Upon learning the tests results, I had said, "Thank God." Later, I realized that I had simply used it as a common phrase. My little five-year old daughter was talking to God with an appreciative heart.

Later, as I was tucking Todd in for the night, he asked, "Mom, if God made Angela well, why didn't he make me well?" I tried to explain that her first tests had been incorrect; that she had been misdiagnosed. I told him that sometimes children were born blind, and they helped others to appreciate their ability to see; some people were born deaf, and they helped others appreciate their hearing; some cannot walk, and they help us appreciate our healthy legs. I continued that perhaps God wanted him to help

LaRecea Gibbs

others appreciate their healthy lungs; that perhaps God had a special job for him to do that he could do better by having CF; but how could I explain to a seven-year-old why he had to be sick when I could not understand myself? Once again I asked, "God, why Todd?"

Todd was the first child in our entire county to be diagnosed with cystic fibrosis. He had just begun first grade. Most people were like us and had never heard of CF. Soon they learned that it is genetic and fatal. The news spread quickly in our small community. They reacted with love and concern, but I was afraid his classmates would overhear their parents talking and treat Todd differently.

I decided the best way to confront that problem was to speak to his class and answer their questions with facts and honesty. We never tried to hide the fact that Todd had a serious illness, but emphasized that it was only a *part* of Todd. It was not *who* he was. I went to his classroom and Todd and I talked about CF. Actually, Todd did most of the talking. He explained he would be coughing a lot, but his classmates could not catch anything from him. He showed them how we did percussion and described the mist tent under which he slept each night. We answered each question his six year old classmates had, and that was the end of it. We took the mystery away from this new mysterious disease. We tried to treat CF as if it was no big deal. In return, his classmates did the same.

I have talked to parents whose CF children have had a very different school experience. Many have said their children were taunted, made to feel different, or simply ignored by their fellow students. Often their school years were difficult. Some parents said they were afraid their child would be shunned if their illness became public knowledge. Todd never experienced that. Perhaps it was our honesty from the beginning. I believe when children are not given the facts or told the truth, their imagination often makes the situation worse. We gave the gift of honesty, and in return, we received the gifts of acceptance and compassion.

When Todd was seven, he was chosen as Kentucky's Cystic Fibrosis Poster Child. He met with the governor and represented the state CF foundation in its fund raising campaigns. He spoke to groups at fundraisers. He surprised people with the way he could speak in front of audiences.

Now, I had a new dream, to find a cure for CF in Todd's lifetime.

I was working on a style show for a CF fundraiser. Driving home one afternoon after a meeting, Todd asked a question I was not prepared to answer. He had met several other children with CF in the hospital who later died. He asked if CF killed children. I explained that, yes, CF did sometimes kill just as many other diseases did, such as cancer. I reminded him of a neighbor who had beaten cancer and explained that was why I was working so hard for the foundation, so they could find a cure.

That answer seemed sufficient to his seven-year-old mind. I had been honest with him. I had also given him the impression that CF did not affect him as it did other children. Later, I realized that, although I was unprepared to answer his question, God had given me the right words. I had answered truthfully, yet given him the belief that CF would not destroy him. Later, at age eleven, Todd asked if *he* was going to die after he learned of DK's death. That question was much more difficult to answer.

QUALITY OR QUANTITY?

At first, Todd was often hospitalized. The doctors suggested we remove him from public school, hoping to avoid illnesses that he might catch from his classmates. His grandmother was his first grade teacher, and she felt she could teach him as well at home in a safer environment, but Todd loved school and his classmates. Even at that young age, he displayed the characteristic of being determined to live a *normal* life in spite of CF.

His father and I agreed we had rather Todd live a full, active life and die young and happy, than live a sheltered, longer life where he was not really permitted to live at all. We decided we would let him do all the things other kids did, even though, at that time, it really was not an approved approach for CF patients. Neither the doctors nor we knew that difficult decision would prove to be one of the things that actually enabled him to live longer. Now doctors encourage that approach. It was a decision we never doubted and one for which Todd often thanked us.

When a person spends so much time away from family and friends, some of the persons one meets at the hospital often become close friends. I remember the first time I met Sissy and her mother, Sue. It was during one of Todd's early hospitalizations. No one in our community knew very much about CF at that time. Our family and friends were supportive, but no one could understand how it felt to know that we could lose our child at any time. He looked so healthy and was so active, it was difficult for our friends and family to realize the seriousness of the disease. Only another mother of a CF child could truly understand. That is one reason my friendship with Sue became so important to me. I called her "my hospital sister."

Families of sick children often gathered in the waiting room to take a break away from their child. I think friendships are quickly made because of the common bond of having a very ill child. Sue was the mother of Sissy who also had cystic fibrosis. Todd and Sissy were often hospitalized at the same time. Sissy was younger than Todd was and her disease more advanced.

Many times when we arrived at UK Medical Center, Sissy would already be there. She would be staying in the bed, rarely outside her room unless she was in a wheelchair, and not eating. Within a few days, she and Todd would be walking all over the hospital floor, in each other's room, visiting the gift shop, and making late-night trips to the snack bar. Sue and I made many trips to Baskin Robbins. A parent will try anything to get a sick child to eat when he has no appetite.

Todd thought he was the reason Sissy's condition improved. He thought he could always make her feel better. If Sue was "my hospital sister," Sissy became Todd's "hospital best friend."

Todd and Sissy were hospitalized at the same time when she died. Sissy had been in the hospital for a lengthy period of time when we took Todd for a routine check-up. Dr. Wilson found a new infection and decided to admit Todd. However, there were no available beds on the pediatric floor. While waiting, Todd learned that Sissy was there and very ill. In fact, she was so ill they had kept the other bed in her room vacant. When Todd saw how sick Sissy was, he begged to be admitted in her room. He was certain he could have her up and about in a few days. The admitting resident was horrified at the suggestion. They never placed a boy and girl together at their ages. I believe they were around the ages of nine and eleven.

Todd was not going to give up. Someone had to make Sissy keep fighting. He knew he was that person. He located the Chief of Pediatrics, a kind, loving, gifted doctor. Although she had never treated either Todd or Sissy, because of their frequent hospitalizations, she knew both well. She always had time to stop and chat with Todd whenever she met him in the hall.

Todd pleaded his case. Sissy was going to die if something was not done. He had lost other friends to CF, but he was determined not to lose his best CF friend. She agreed with Todd. She was one who cared more about the patient than the rules. She ordered the resident to admit Todd into the room with Sissy.

After several days, it became apparent to everyone that Sissy was not going to survive. They moved Todd to another wing. After her death, Todd refused to get close to any other patient until his late teens.

FREQUENT
HOSPITALIZATIONS

Todd's hospitalizations became more frequent. During his seventh grade year, he was in the hospital a total of fourteen weeks; his eighth grade, seventeen weeks. We would sometimes go for what we thought was a routine check-up only to learn Todd had a new infection and would need to be hospitalized. It became necessary to keep a packed suitcase in the trunk of the car. I stopped making long-term plans and began living day-to-day.

It was difficult living that life. There were times I would arise in the morning expecting my usual daily activities only to end the day in Lexington in the hospital. Todd rarely complained of feeling sick, so unless I watched carefully, his infections would advance to the point he needed IV meds before I even knew he was becoming ill. Since Todd was usually good-natured, if he became irritable or had a low-grade temperature, I knew that was a clue he had a new infection. A few times, I took him to the doctor and could only tell the physician that something just was not right and an x-ray would show a new pneumonia.

In spite of the frequent hospitalizations, Todd was doing well in school, playing Little League baseball, even making the All-Star team, and playing basketball.

By this time, research had shown that the mist tent did not actually help the CF patient and was even possibly harmful. Doctors removed it from the treatment plan. Todd was very open about his disease believing that it was his responsibility to tell others about CF, so they would want to give to the foundation.

He might not be able to control the killer, but he hoped that research would find a control or cure in his lifetime. He spoke about CF at school, clubs, CF parent functions, and later as a teen, he spoke to the medical students at UK.

CYSTIC FIBROSIS AFFECTS THE ENTIRE FAMILY

Todd was conscious, even as a child, that CF was probably as hard on his sisters as it was on him. Once, he was hospitalized on Angela's birthday. I had planned a slumber party for twelve of her friends when he became ill. I was going to reschedule the party, but Todd insisted I leave him alone, go home and have the party as planned. He said "Remember, Mom, I'm just one of your children, although we both know the most important. [Todd's sense of humor again] I know I take a lot of your attention when I am sick. I'm sorry about that, but you will not miss Angela's birthday."

Another time, he insisted I leave him to go home for a style show in which Angela and Hope were modeling dresses I had sewn for them. He told me years later that the reason he often disappeared to his room or walking on our farm after a hospitalization was so I could focus extra attention on the girls.

One time, while taking a break in the hospital's waiting room, I met a young woman who was visiting a cousin. She had a brother who had died from CF. As we talked, she spoke about CF from a sibling's viewpoint. She said her mother focused only on her brother while he was alive. His siblings felt ignored, angry, and hurt. When he died, the mother could not understand why she did not have a relationship with her other children. She had not only lost a son to CF, she had lost all of her children because of her reaction to CF. I promised myself that I would not allow that to happen to me. It dawned on me that day that I could lose Angela or Hope in an accident or some other illness before I lost Todd. I think I actually enjoyed each of my children more because cystic fibrosis taught me that we are only guaranteed the moment we have.

I always remembered the conversation with that young woman. I tried very hard to give all my children the same amount of attention when we were home. Did I succeed? You would have to ask my daughters that question.

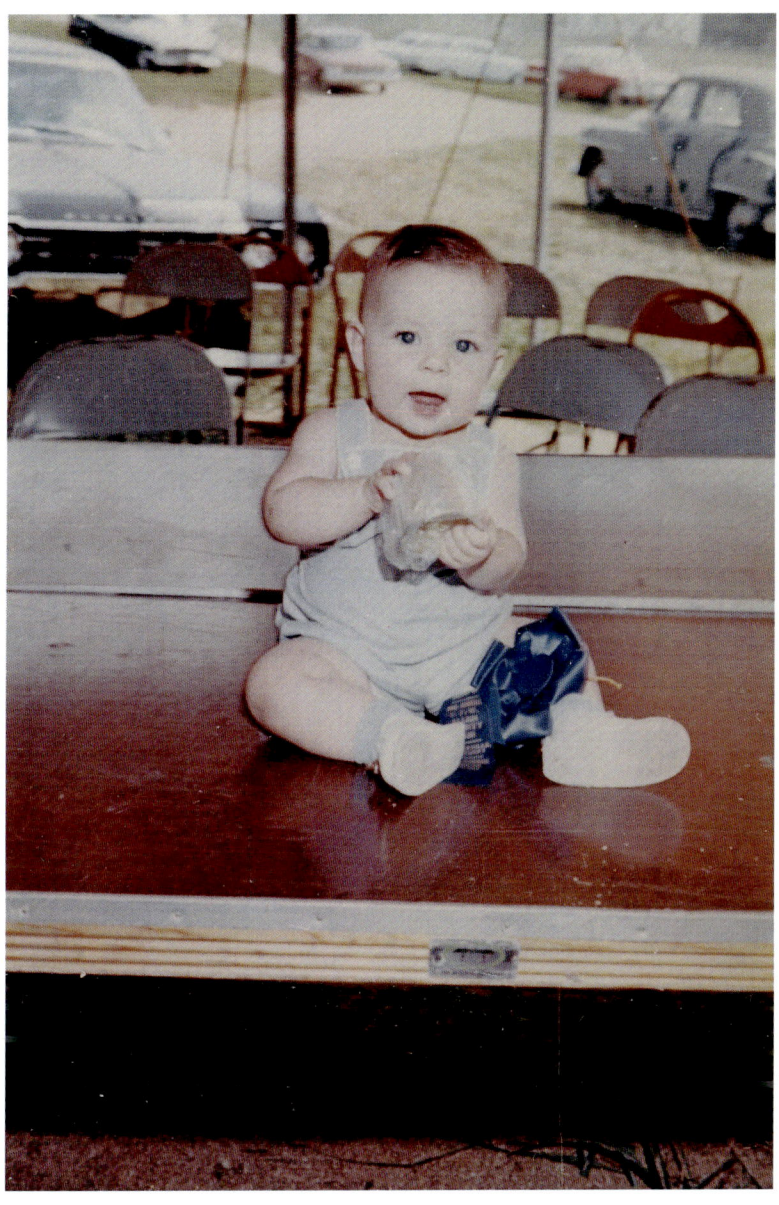

Todd, age nine months, won first place in the baby contest and was named "Little Mr. Allen County 1965." It was at this time that symptoms began that we later learned were symptoms of cystic fibrosis.

Todd age eighteen months

LaRecea Gibbs

Todd age four modeling at a fashion show

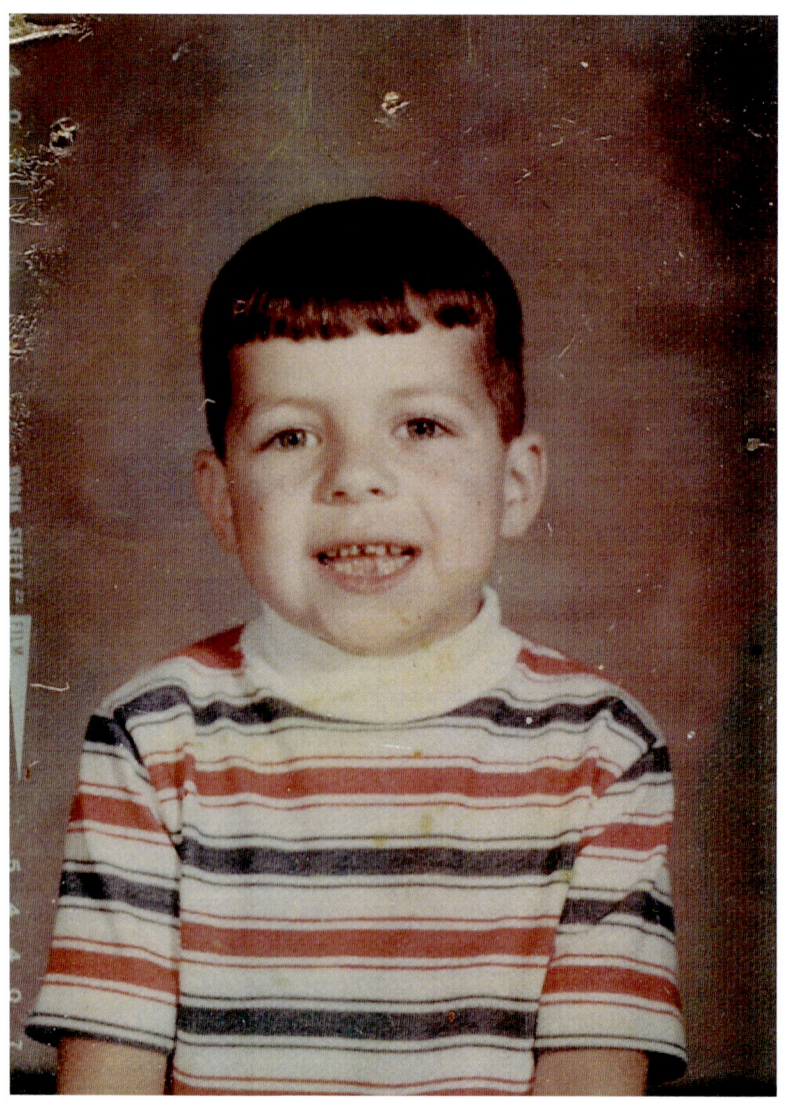

Todd's first grade picture, three months after his CF diagnosis

LaRecea Gibbs

Todd is holding the championship trophy when the Lady Patriots won the regional championship 1979. He was the trainer and very proud to be part of the team. That win enabled them to go to the state tournament.

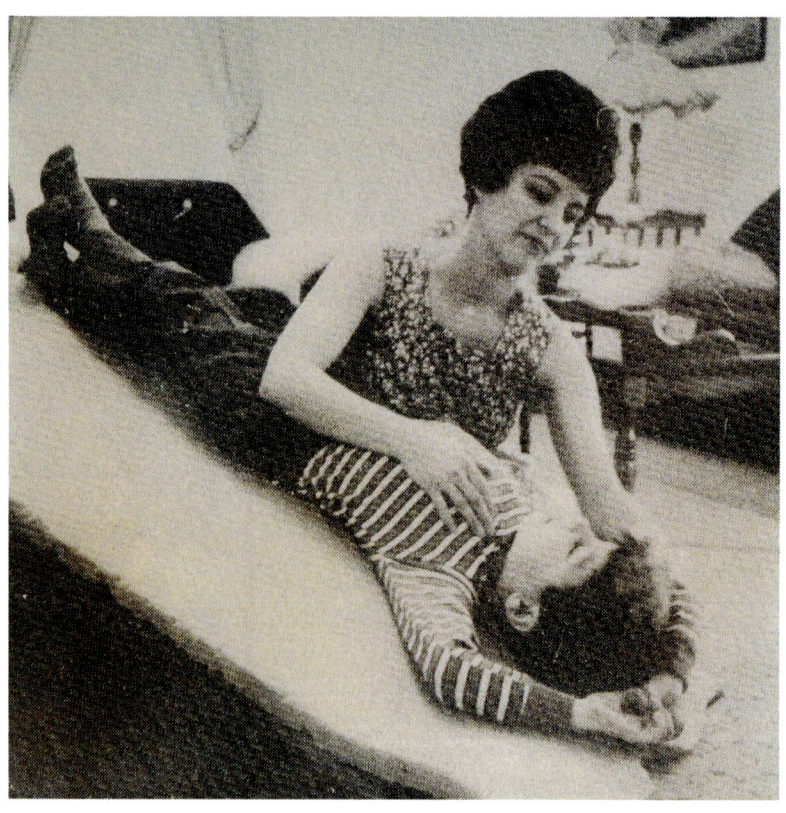

Mom doing Todd's (age six) postural drainage which we did twice a day for forty-five minutes. It was difficult when school was in session.

LaRecea Gibbs

Todd and his sisters were clowning around in their Christmas outfits that I made. Hope, three, Todd, nine, Angela, seven.

Not a Wasted Breath

Todd, age nine, was selected to be on the All-Star team. He played shortstop.

LaRecea Gibbs

Todd is sitting on the shoulders of championship team members, Vera Hall and Donna Smith. After seeing this, his father understood why he chose to be manager of the girls' team instead of working with the boys. Although he was fourteen, he looked much younger. (Used with permission of the National Cystic Fibrosis Foundation)

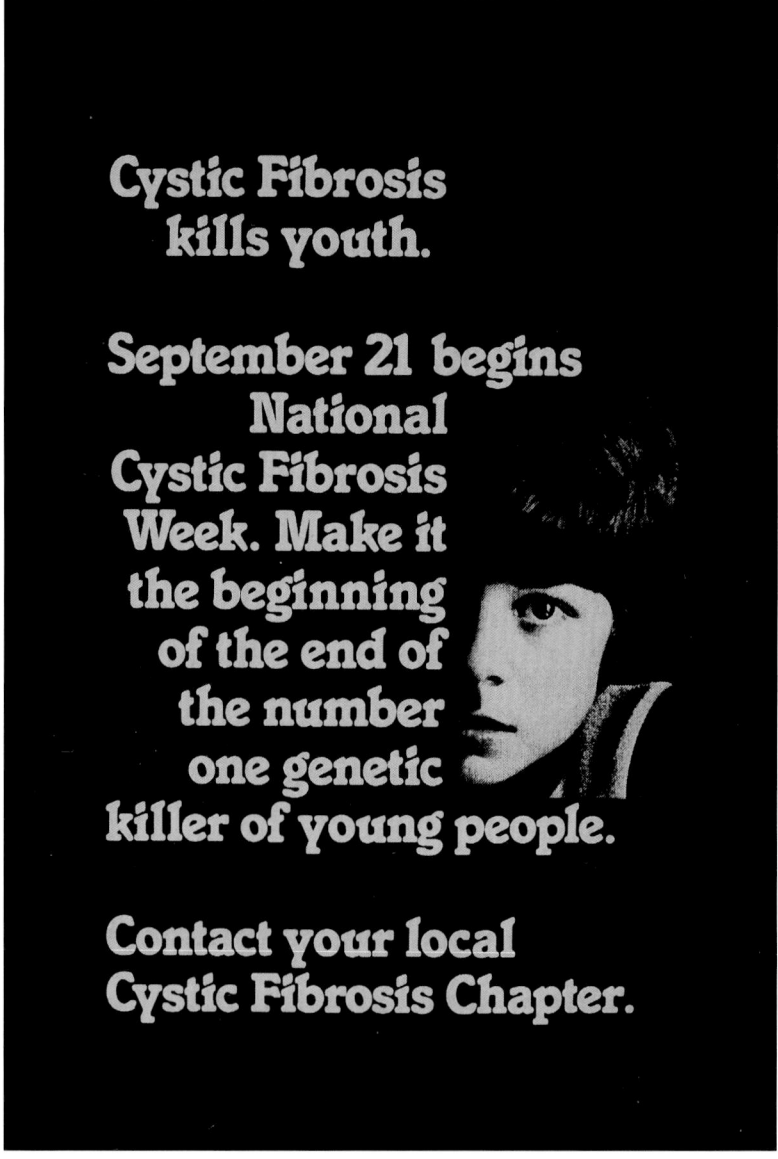

This poster was used when Todd was "National Cystic Fibrosis Representative 1980-1981." (Used with permission of the National Cystic Fibrosis Foundation)

La Recea Gibbs

"An apple a day will not keep the doctor away when one has cystic fibrosis." (Used with permission of the National Cystic Fibrosis Foundation)

Todd is at school doing his IV's. He came up with the idea of using the large syringe instead of having to push an IV pole through the school hall as he earlier did. (Used with permission of the National Cystic Fibrosis Foundation)

           LaRecea Gibbs

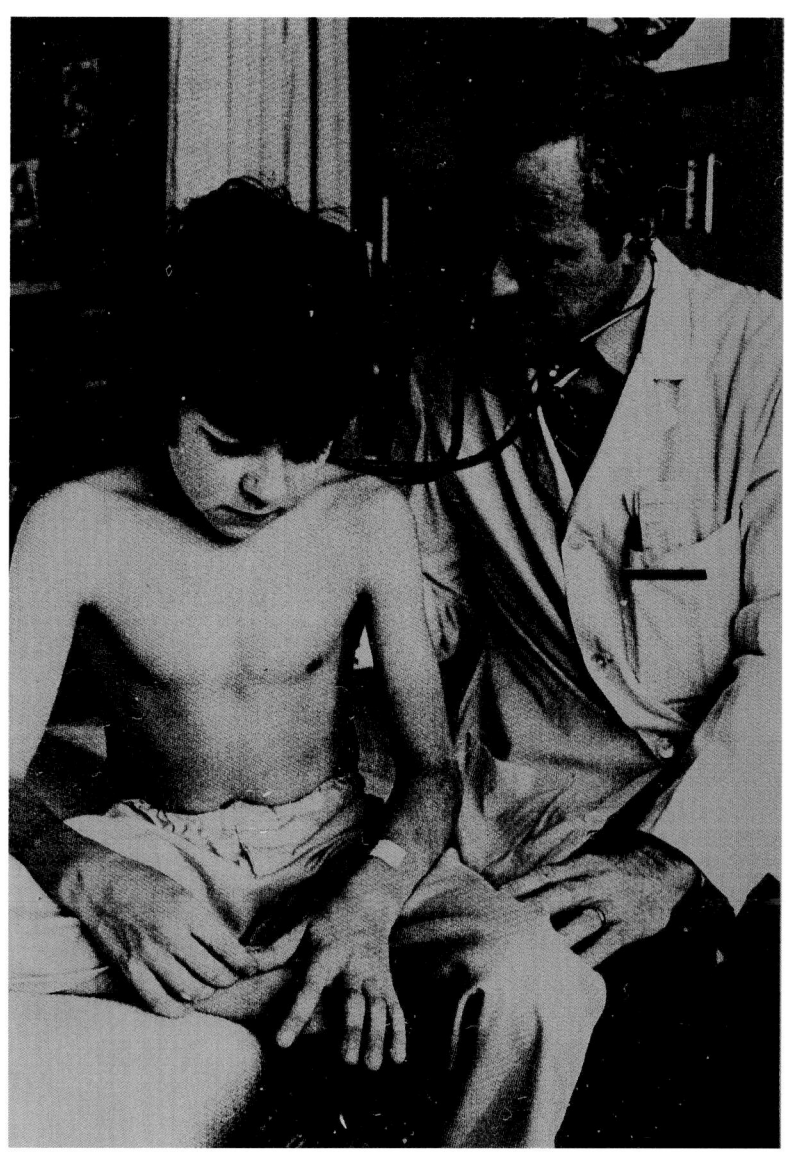

Todd with his CF doctor, David Wilson, MD, director of the University of Kentucky's CF clinic. (Used with permission of the National Cystic Fibrosis Foundation)

Not a Wasted Breath

*Todd, age fifteen, was always smiling. (Used with permission of the
National Cystic Fibrosis Foundation)*

LaRecea Gibbs

Our family meets President Jimmy Carter in the Oval Office. Todd was the "National Cystic Fibrosis Poster Representative, 1980-81." (Used with permission of the National Cystic Fibrosis Foundation)

Todd shakes the President's hand. Todd was fifteen years old when we went to Washington although he looks much younger. (Used with permission of the National Cystic Fibrosis Foundation)

LaRecea Gibbs

The President seemed pleased with the University of Kentucky ball shirt autographed by star player, Kyle Macy. (Used with permission of the National Cystic Fibrosis Foundation)

Todd watches as President Carter autographs a booklet, "The History of the White House" for him. Todd noticed a worn Bible on the President's desk and was deeply impressed. (Used with permission of the National Cystic Fibrosis Foundation)

LaRecea Gibbs

During Todd's senior year, he played the cymbals for the Allen County Scottsville High School marching, pep, and concert bands.

Todd's senior picture.

LaRecea Gibbs

Todd with close friends, Howard Ives and Todd Hurt.

After graduation, and only eighteen years old, Todd bought this house. He lived there until his death.

LaRecea Gibbs

Todd, twenty-one, Angela, nineteen, and Hope, fifteen had this picture made for me as a Christmas surprise.

Todd at work at the radio station where he was News Director and known as "Scoop."

LaRecea Gibbs

Todd was a son, a big brother, and the protector of our family.

Todd was a certified Kentucky basketball official. He sometimes refereed four varsity games a week in spite of having only thirty percent lung capacity.

LaRecea Gibbs

Todd did play by play of the girls' games for WVLE radio. Seated next to him is Donnie Meador, one of his closest friends, who kept stats for the games.

*The "two Todds" were best friends from first grade until their deaths.
Gibbs, almost eight inches shorter than Hurt, is standing on a box, the
only time he is Hurt's height. Hurt had hemophilia and died twenty-
two months after Gibbs.*

Mom is holding the Bible as Todd takes the oath of office for his first term as Scottsville city council member. He was reelected for a second term and was serving at the time of his death. Also pictured is his paternal grandmother, Ovaleta Gibbs.

Todd, age twenty–nine, receiving his BA degree from President Thomas Meredith, Western Kentucky University

LaRecea Gibbs

Our last family photo was taken on Todd's wedding day December 16, 1994. Ten months later on that exact date, Todd's casket sat on the same spot for his funeral. Left to right is Angela, Todd, Mom, and Hope.

HOSPITAL STAFF
AND FUN

After getting a patient stabilized in the hospital, the protocol was to give the child a pass to leave the hospital for brief periods to go out to dinner, see a movie, etc. Doctors realized that a child who was spending so much time in the hospital needed some periods of normalcy. Todd had become such a favorite of the doctors, nurses, and other staff members, that it was often one of them who took him out on pass while I waited at the hospital.

Once, two of Todd's nurses and his resident asked to take Todd on pass to a movie. It was in 3-D, and they thought it would be a new experience for him. Well, it certainly turned out to be different for him, but not the way they planned! They returned embarrassed and apologizing. Unknown to them, the movie was R rated, far too mature for a boy Todd's age. Todd said hands kept going over his eyes the entire movie. We all had a good laugh, and they sighed with relief at my reaction.

He also developed a close friendship with one of his respiratory therapists, LaDawn. She not only did her job professionally, she added much happiness to his life and often "rescued" him from the hospital for a break.

TRUE BLUE UK
WILDCAT FAN

Todd and Dr. Wilson shared a common passion for the UK Wildcats' basketball team. Several times, Dr. Wilson gave him his tickets if he was going to be on call. At that period, UK was one of the most successful teams in the country, and it was difficult to get tickets. As a staff member of UK, it was much easier for doctors to get tickets. Todd attended many of the top games during his hospitalizations, even going into the dressing room once after a game to meet UK's star player, Sam Bowie. Kyle Macy was his all-time favorite player. Dr. Wilson's nurse attended the same church as Joe Hall, UK's coach. She told him about Todd's hero worship of Kyle. Soon after, Kyle came to the hospital to visit. The whole wing of pediatrics-nurses, doctors, patients, and their families-became excited when word spread of Kyle's impending visit. He was just as nice as Todd expected, and it was the best medicine Todd could have received.

Todd saw so many of UK's big games that it became a joke among his friends. "Hey, Todd, a big game is coming up. Are you feeling sick?"

THE MIDDLE SCHOOL YEARS

By the time Todd was eleven, he was hospitalized because of pneumonia at least once every three months. Hospitalizations had become a big part of our lives. A few times, the hospitalization was as short as ten days, sometimes a month or longer. Usually it was a three-week period of treatment.

When Todd developed pneumonia, he required IV medicines; IV's meant hospitalization; hospitalization meant I had to put the girls' lives on hold while I stayed at the hospital with Todd. It often came unexpectedly. We would be living a *normal* life, and then suddenly we would be packing to be gone to live our other life.

We managed to maintain a somewhat normal home life until acute illness occurred. Then our lives were turned upside down. One of the hardest parts was leaving my two young daughters, knowing I would be away from them for several weeks with only brief visits.

Hope was five and Angela nine when the frequent hospitalizations began. I can remember rushing through the house trying to pack, not only for Todd, but also for Donald and me. We would be gone for an undetermined amount of time. That also meant I had to pack for the girls who would be staying with Donald's parents. Following behind was often Hope, crying and begging me not to leave her again. My heart tore between the desire to provide my girls with a normal childhood and the need to be with Todd. I knew what CF was doing to Todd's health, but

I often worried about what it was doing to the emotional health of the girls.

We were fortunate to be blessed with Donald's parents who stepped in and became more than grandparents when he was ill. Mrs. Gibbs taught first grade but never hesitated to care for the girls when needed.

In spite of all the hospitalizations, Todd had an unusual record of attendance at school. He never missed a single day unless he was in the hospital. That winter had been a rough one for our part of Kentucky. We had so much snow that year that schools closed for a record number of days. During one three-week hospitalization, Todd only missed three days of actual school.

Todd began his seventh grade. He was elected student body president and became manager for both the girls' and boys' basketball teams. Realizing his short stature would prevent him from being a basketball player past Little League, Todd looked for another way to overcome that obstacle. He was never one to stop because there was an obstacle in his path. He merely looked for a way around it. Being a manager was the next best thing to playing and, as usual, Todd put his whole heart and soul in it.

The girls' basketball coach at the middle school was also coach at the high school. He became impressed with Todd's attitude and willingness to work extra hard at whatever he attempted. He told him he could be manager of the varsity team when he entered high school the next year. Todd later attended a camp at Western Kentucky University that taught him the necessary skills needed to become a certified trainer. He wrapped ankles, iced injuries, and, usually wearing a suit and tie, sat next to Coach Young on the bench. That was the beginning of a very special relationship with David Young. He first became his mentor, later friend, sometimes a father figure, and later a groomsman in his wedding.

Once, Donald asked Todd why he wanted to be involved with the girls' team instead of working with boys' basketball. Later in the season, Donald had his answer when he saw two of the star players carrying Todd on their shoulders. Since Todd was so small, people sometimes forgot he was fourteen not the ten he looked.

The girls' team had three things Todd especially liked. They were ranked in the top of Kentucky's girls' basketball teams, David Young was the coach, and along with their athleticism, they were pretty!

THE FINANCIAL
COSTS OF CF

I feared each hospitalization might be the type of pneumonia resistant to the antibiotics. We saw it happen so many times with other cystic fibrosis children with whom we had become close.

Both Donald and I often stayed at the hospital with Todd in the beginning. It was a long drive and until Todd stabilized, Donald wanted to be close. Since he was a farmer, he could arrange his time to be with us.

There were no private rooms on the pediatric floor at that time, and the Ronald McDonald houses were just being established and were not available in our area. We slept in a chair in the lobby or placed a blanket on the floor beside Todd's bed.

Cystic fibrosis can be a very financially draining illness. In spite of the need to be together during an illness, financial difficulties often become a big focus in the lives of CF patients and their families. Medicines and treatments are very expensive. As in our case, families must sometimes travel long distances in order to receive treatment at a CF clinic instead of being treated by a local physician. Since statistics show that patients have a longer survival rate when under the care of a CF clinic, families are willing to make the sacrifice for their child.

Although we had insurance, our out-of-pocket expenses were running approximately eight to ten thousand dollars a year, and that was in the 1970's. I was doing substitute teaching, but because of the unpredictability of our life, I was unable to work fulltime. We really needed the income. That is often the case in

CF families. Sometimes parents face the possibility of not only losing their child but also their home in order to fight for their child's life.

Unlike some other diseases where there will be enormous medical bills for a period of time then the patient gets well or dies, CF means years of large medical bills the patient's entire life. My family did not take vacations, the children did not wear brand label clothes, and often it was a stretch to pay for cheerleading camps, music lessons, or gymnastics, etc. I worried how it would affect the girls. Now I look back and think it may have had a positive influence on their lives.

Each of my three children paid for most of their college by working, sometimes two or more part-time jobs in addition to taking full semester loads. Each graduated in four years with outstanding point averages. I do not intend to brag, but if I sound proud, I plead guilty.

Angela graduated first with a degree in public relations. She works in advertising and marketing and is recognized for her work ethic, creativeness, and discipline. She is married to Craig Martin and is the mother of one son, Connor.

Hope received her degree in broadcasting and television and worked in special events until the birth of her first son. Now she is a stay-at-home mom and the mother of Calister, Alex, and Will Turner. She is married to Patrick Cummiskey and has two stepchildren, Jackson and Ansley. She is my Martha Stewart.

Todd also graduated with a degree in television and broadcasting while working three jobs and, at the time of his death, was working toward a master's degree.

My children sometimes went without many of the material advantages of their friends, but they always had one thing in abundance—my love. Both girls are outstanding mothers and women.

Cystic fibrosis brought some hard times to our family, but I believe those experiences may have molded my daughters into the women they are today.

MAKING HOSPITALIZATIONS EASIER

Long hospitalizations can be boring for an active child like Todd. Whenever he had a special event he was anticipating, it seemed he ended up in the hospital. He never allowed CF to become the focus of his life, unless he was in the hospital. Then he would become depressed for the first two or three days.

In a later conversation with Todd when he was in his middle twenties, I told him that the way he coped with CF was unreal, almost superhuman. I had spoken to other patients living with the disease, and they felt and lived completely different than Todd did. I asked him if he was really that strong or if he was just a good actor. He answered, "Mom, if I was that good of an actor, I'd be in Hollywood instead of sitting here on the couch talking to you." He continued explaining that the ones to whom I had spoken allowed CF to become the focus of their lives. That, he would never do! If he did, then cystic fibrosis would win even before it killed him. He said he did not live his life thinking about and fearing what CF could do. The only time he became angry or depressed was when he was hospitalized or one of his friends died from CF. When two of his closest friends died on the same day, he was devastated.

Hospitalizations were not always a negative thing. I searched for things that would make them less boring. One hospitalization, I got Todd a goldfish. After a few days, the fish began looking sick, floating near the top. [I had many goldfish funerals while my children were growing up.] Todd and his resident were discussing the upcoming demise of the fish. The resident decided the fish would benefit from additional oxygen. They could not just turn on the oxygen by Todd's bed without a written order, so the doctor wrote an order for oxygen on Todd's chart. Soon the respiratory therapist arrived, concerned. She knew Todd had never used oxygen before. She was a friend of Todd's and was concerned his condition had worsened. When she learned that the order was for Todd's fish, not him, she was greatly relieved. The news spread, and everyone had a good laugh. This was just an example of how everyone at UK treated Todd. Our experiences with the staff made those days and weeks bearable.

I often went shopping for crafts that Todd and I could do together and anything to read related to the space shuttle. That and basketball were two of Todd's passions. Once when I asked him about his future goals, he stated he wanted to be the ABC news anchor and fly to space, then added, "Now realistically ... "

During one hospitalization, Lexington received eighteen inches of snow. Many of the medical staff were stranded at the hospital and others could not get to the hospital to relieve them.

Todd was bored, so I went outside and gathered snow for Todd and his roommate to make snowmen. I ended up having to make several trips since Todd's room became the snowman designing area. Doctors and nurses joined in the fun trying to be the most creative. The snowmen did not last long in the heated room, but it took their minds off the terrible storm for a short period.

Todd rarely stayed in his room after the first few days. He would be visiting the floor pharmacist or doctors, nurses, or other patients. Fourth floor pediatrics was divided into three wings. He especially enjoyed visiting the baby and toddler wing. One little two-year-old boy became a favorite. He had been in the hospital since birth. His mother lived in the mountains of Eastern Kentucky, had several other children, and because of lack of transportation, she was unable to visit very often. Whenever the child saw Todd, he began jumping, laughing, and reaching his hands for Todd to take him. One day I returned to the room to find Todd and a friend entertaining the little boy in Todd's bed. Alarmed that the nurses might be looking for the child, [they were frantic] I took him back to his room. From that point on, Todd did his visiting and entertainment of babies on the wing!

Todd sometimes went with his doctor on rounds. During several hospitalizations, he visited a little girl his age that was in a coma because of a car accident. He would stand beside her bed and talk to her as if she could answer. Her dad encouraged the visits. He was convinced she could hear and would eventually recover. The medical staff and I felt sorry for the dad's unrealistic expectations, but I allowed Todd to continue his visits each time he was hospitalized. After several months, the child came out of the coma. She told her dad that she remembered a little boy visiting and talking to her. During a routine clinic visit, as we exited the elevator, there sat the little girl in her wheelchair with her dad. When she heard Todd speak, she said, "There's the boy I was telling you about, Daddy."

I not only tried to make Todd's hospitalizations easier for him, he tried to do the same for me. Sometimes people asked how we managed to cope with Todd being so sick so often. Todd often helped us instead of the other way around. One Easter is an example of his concern for me. We had been in Lexington for three weeks and were expecting to go home for Easter. As the time approached, x-rays showed that a new infection had developed, and we would need to stay for another ten day round of medicine. I went into the lobby to call home. When my daughters learned we would not be together for Easter, they began to cry. After I hung up the phone, I, too, began to cry. I looked up and standing down the hall was Todd watching with concern. The next day, I received a corsage of two cymbidium orchids to wear for Easter. Todd had used money he had received in get-well cards to buy my flowers instead of buying something for himself in the gift shop. Seeing how touched I was, he said, "I bet you would have been just as happy with one flower. I should have saved the extra money and bought something for me." He continued that he had asked Dr. Wilson for an Easter pass, and Dr. Wilson had invited us to his church. Afterwards, we went to eat. It was one of my most memorable Easters ever!

Regardless of my worry and concern about Todd's health, whenever the UK Medical Center came into view, I began to relax. I felt everything would be okay. We spent so much time there it was almost like visiting family. The staff at UK gave us much more than medicine. They gave us friendship and hope.

When I chaired a bike-a-thon fundraiser for the CF foundation, several doctors and nurses made the one hundred sixty mile drive to ride and show their support. Todd was hospitalized until a week before the event. Riders received pledges based on each mile they rode, and Todd used his time in the hospital to raise most of his money. One intern pledged a dollar for each mile Todd rode. No one expected Todd to ride more than ten miles after his lengthy hospitalization, but he rode thirty-three miles!

MISCHIEF AND MIRACLES

Todd often had an old friend in the hospital when he was there. If not, he made a new one. He found ways to have fun, some of which I did not know until years later.

[The following is an excerpt from his weekly column *Scoop sounds off*]

NEWSPAPER ARTICLE

Many wild things have happened at UK. Once, my roommate, Roddy, and I went to see if we could find the laboratory animals in the basement. We waited until midnight so no one would be around. Well, we found the animals, but we also found more than we wanted. After wandering into a dark room, Roddy turned on the light to find we were in the room where medical students worked on cadavers. We left *quickly* and never went back to see the little animals.

Then there was the time I wrecked during an IV pole race. Both bottles of fluids fell onto the floor and broke. I cried, the nurse felt sorry for me, and I didn't get in trouble. Everything worked out for the best. But from then on, they used plastic bags instead of the glass bottles of fluids. The IV pole races continued.

Todd almost died the summer of his thirteenth year. We were trying to keep him at our small rural hospital, so I could be close to the girls and maintain some semblance of a normal life. He had been in the hospital for two weeks and was getting worse. He was not responding to any of the treatments.

I suggested to our family physician that we transfer Todd to Lexington. He had been in regular contact with the Lexington clinic. He said they were doing everything possible that UK could do and reminded me that I had known for seven years that this time was coming.

My brother was in a hospital in the nearby county with a massive heart attack and not expected to live. Donald was in the hospital in Tennessee facing back surgery. With Todd so ill, our family doctor thought it was advisable that we be close to home, supported by family and friends.

Each day, I watched Todd grow progressively worse. Finally, I removed him from the hospital and, together with the girls, headed to Lexington. When Dr. Wilson viewed Todd's x-ray, he agreed with our family doctor. One lung was completely full of infection, and the other was almost as bad.

He told me that we were facing the moment we had so feared. I should call Donald, because we needed to be together. Since the girls were with me and I needed to get Donald out of the hospital and pack our clothes, Dr. Wilson allowed Todd to return home with us for the night.

I cannot describe the emotions I was feeling. There was so much to do. I was alone with the three children, so I had to put on my brave face. Yet, I knew I was possibly facing the last night we would all be together at home. I called my pastor, Dr. Ron Bradley. He asked if I wanted him to pray with me. I answered, "You pray and I'll drive. I just can't pray right now."

The drive home that I had so dreaded actually became a pleasant trip. None of the children knew what the doctor had said, and for them, it was just another hospitalization. I listened as they discussed summer plans and argued where they wanted to eat.

That night, after everyone was asleep, I was trying to pack and arrange for what lay ahead. The impact of the day's events really hit me. I could not function. I had always prayed for strength and courage to accept whatever we were facing, instead of asking God to do what I wanted. On that night, I prayed a different prayer. I went into the front yard and kneeled under a big oak tree, sobbing. I pleaded with God to let Todd live just one more year so we could grant his three big wishes.

Todd had three things he wanted very badly: he wanted to go to Disney World; [we did not take vacations because of the large medical bills] he wanted a baby calf of his own to raise and had already prepared the barn stall; and he was excitingly anticipating being girls' basketball manager at the high school. I promised God if he would allow Todd to have those three things, I would not question him when he took Todd.

After the prayer, I felt peaceful and accomplished everything I needed to do by the early morning. Then Donald, Todd, and I left for the hospital.

Upon our arrival at the CF clinic, Dr. Wilson sent for Todd's x-ray to show Donald. He wanted him to understand what we were facing. The x-ray was misplaced, so he ordered another one. They had always told us that it took five days of medications before improvement would show on an x-ray. Todd had not received any medicine, so no changes were expected.

Imagine everyone's surprise when the x-ray showed significant improvement from the day before. When they found the first x-ray and compared it to the second one, everyone was amazed. Todd's doctor had no explanation. Three weeks later, Todd left the hospital.

That fall, we experienced a horrifying scare with Todd's health. I had a long-term substitute teaching position, so Donald was staying with Todd at the hospital. One afternoon at school, I received a call from Dr. Wilson. Todd was hemorrhaging from his lungs. This was not the usual spitting up blood when a blood vessel bursts after a severe coughing spell. None of the staff had seen this amount of blood before from a CF patient. He had coughed and a large amount of blood came gushing forth. I later learned from Todd that the room was full of doctors and nurses, watching with concern and amazement, as Dr. Wilson discussed with his team what they could try.

I began the long journey alone breaking all the speed limits. Actually, it was the one and only time I hoped to be stopped by a police officer. There were always many state police on the interstate. They had stopped me for speeding too often not to notice. I did not know if Todd was dead or alive. This was before the time of cell phones. I hoped the police could radio someone at UK and learn Todd's condition, but no such luck.

When I arrived at the hospital, I learned that the bleeding had stopped, but he was running a fever of one hundred four degrees. This was high for anyone, but especially Todd. Even when he had pneumonia, Todd's temperature was usually never higher than one hundred. I have been told that a cystic fibroses patient's body is so accustomed to infections that it does not react as other bodies do.

I really understood the seriousness of the situation when Dr. Wilson returned to the hospital around midnight, just to check on Todd. He improved more slowly than usual. That hospitalization lasted a month.

That Christmas, my brother, L.C., who is a farmer, gave Todd a calf. No one had told him about Todd's wish or my prayer. *Could this be God's work?* I wondered.

A few weeks later, Donald's sister, Dianna, called to invite us to go with her family to Disney World. Her husband won the trip from his company because of his high sales. It included a condominium large enough for both families. We would be cooking many of our meals in the condominium's kitchen, so our major expense would be the park tickets and our gas. We eagerly accepted her invitation. Another of Todd's wishes was granted.

The following school year, Todd became girls' basketball trainer at the high school. He did not miss a single game! Remarkable, since he was hospitalized so often in the past.

Todd's last big wish was fulfilled. My desperate prayer to God that night was answered. I was so afraid Todd would die then. Afterwards, I always felt that each year Todd lived was a bonus gift from God.

LaRecea Gibbs

LEARNING TO
DO HOME IV'S

Todd's best friend from first grade and until his death was a boy also named Todd. They referred to each other by their last names, Hurt and Gibbs. They looked like Mutt and Jeff together. Hurt was tall for his age while Gibbs was short for his. Hurt had hemophilia, and like Donald and me, his parents were determined that he live a normal life.

The two Todds were as close as brothers, remaining best friends throughout their lives. Both lived similar lives. Hurt married the year after Gibbs. Sadly, he also died twenty-two months after Gibbs. He had hepatitis, the result of blood transfusions needed for his genetic disease. He too, had fought with courage and determination all his life.

When Hurt had an injury, his dad gave him plasma at home through an IV. I wondered if we could give Todd's IV meds at home. Perhaps, it could reduce some of his hospital time. The big difference, which I did not realize at the time, was that Hurt's IV was used just to give the plasma. Then it was removed. Todd's would have to remain for several days and could potentially cause several problems.

I discussed the possibility with Dr. Wilson. We talked about our options when Todd was spending more time in the hospital than out. We all wanted Todd to receive the best medical care possible, but I was becoming concerned that we were spending quality time of Todd's life in order to gain quantity. I worried what that could do to Todd's spirit. Home IV's had never been done at that time in KY, and Dr. Wilson knew of only two other CF patients who had tried it.

Dr. Wilson was a very special doctor to us for several years before leaving as CF director. I wish every parent of an ill child could have the support of a physician like him. He treated us as partners in Todd's medical care. From the beginning, he explained to Donald, Todd, and me each medicine and procedure. He taught us how to read Todd's x-rays and recognize a new infiltration as opposed to scaring from an old one. It came in handy when Todd became ill, and we had to take him to our local family physicians.

Drs. Halcomb and Oliver had never treated a CF patient before and, at first, found it difficult to believe Todd could read the results of his x-ray. Once, Dr. Halcomb, after examining and doing an x-ray of Todd's lungs, decided he needed to be hospitalized at UK. He was always good at consulting with the CF clinic. He called Dr. Wilson to make the arrangements. Todd had just recently been to Lexington for his regular check-up and had received a good report.

Dr. Wilson asked our family doctor what Todd thought about the x-ray. That question surprised him. He told Dr. Halcomb to let Todd view it then call him back. Skeptically, Dr. Halcomb took Todd to view the x-ray and listened as he spoke to Dr. Wilson on the phone. He listened as Todd used medical terms to describe what he saw. Dr. Halcomb was impressed. After their consultation, they decided a hospitalization was not necessary.

From that moment on, we never had to ask to view his x-rays. Our family doctors automatically took Todd with them when they viewed the results. I am grateful to them for being willing to adapt to a new way of medical treatment. It sometimes prevented our making the long drive to Lexington, needlessly.

Perhaps I should not have been surprised when Dr. Wilson suggested we try home IV's toward the beginning of Todd's freshman year. The plan was for me to learn how to insert the IV, but I was a poor learner. I kept missing, so we thought it was not going to become a possible option. Todd kept insisting that, since he had watched himself stuck so many times, he could do it himself. Everyone agreed that, even if he were able to place an IV in someone else's arm, it would be much more difficult to stick himself.

Todd kept begging to try, and late one night, while sitting at the nurse's station chatting with some interns, residents, and nurses, he conned a resident into allowing him to try on his arm. He was successful on his first attempt and kept sticking IV's into every willing volunteer he could find that night. The next morning, he proudly told Dr. Wilson that he had started several IV's without missing. He was ready to try on himself. As a result, Todd regained some control of the life that CF was beginning to steal.

All the medical staff, nurses, pharmacists, and other doctors were opposed to the idea. In the 1970's, when we began doing the home IV meds, the needle that was used to give intravenous medicine was called a butterfly. It was small and easily came out of the vein, unlike the later improved catheter.

The medical staff began explaining all the things that could go wrong. There was a high risk of infection and clotting. Would we be able to administer the exact dosage of medicine? Only Dr. Wilson and Todd believed we could be successful, and they stood their ground.

Although it had originally been my idea, I was terrified as I listened to all the instructions while the staff assembled the medical supplies we needed for the planned seven days of home treatment. I wished I had never mentioned it. Even sleeping on the floor beside Todd's bed at the hospital, while nurses had the responsibility of giving Todd his meds, seemed a much easier route than doing it myself. However, Todd was excited at the prospect of shorter hospital stays, and I knew I had to try it once.

Todd did the meds while he was awake. If the needle came out of his arm, Todd restarted it. He received an IV med every four hours. The needle was flushed with a solution called heparin, which prevented clotting, before and after each med. In addition, we irrigated the needle every two hours around the clock.

At night, I was responsible. When it came time for Todd's medicine at midnight his first night at home, I panicked. I could not remember if I was doing everything right. I had to wake Todd to get his assurance that I was doing it correctly.

Since I had to get up every two hours, I found myself barely getting back to sleep before needing to wake up again. Sometimes, I was still in a groggy state. The night I missed Todd's IV while trying to flush it, and instead, stuck him in the arm while he was in a deep sleep, became the moment when Todd decided I was a better mom than nurse. That first week home on IV meds was one of the longest of my life.

Later, when hospitals switched to the IV catheter, Todd was unable to restart the IV if it came out of the vein. A local RN and friend, Annetta Shelton, volunteered to be his back up when needed. Regardless of the time, day or night, she was always happy to help. She enabled Todd to continue doing his home meds. She would never accept anything except thanks, so here is a big public thanks, Annetta.

Todd stayed in the hospital until his condition stabilized. Then, he completed his medications at home. The time varied from seven, to ten, to fourteen days, depending on his progress.

First, he was admitted to the hospital. After the infection was identified and cultures showed which medicines would be effective, he was released to complete the medicine at home. Dr. Wilson always made sure that his pneumonia was responding to a particular medicine before he released him.

The school was always very accepting and extremely supportive of Todd. He attended his classes just like every other student, except he had a needle in his arm that was attached to an IV pole. Later, Todd came up with the idea of administrating the drug with a large syringe, slowly pushing it into the vein. That made it less bothersome than rolling an IV pole through the school halls. I doubt if that is done today. With the drug problems facing our schools, the student probably has to go to an office under supervision if he does home IV meds. It became routine for Todd to complete his meds at home.

The PE teacher called once when Todd was on home IV's. She said the students were taking a test of their physical abilities. Even though Todd had a needle in his arm, he was insisting he could do what the other students were doing. She did not want him to try. She was afraid he would hurt himself.

Mrs. Williams assured Todd she would not count that test against him, but Todd was insistent. He never wanted anyone to give him favors or treat him differently because he had CF. She asked what she should do. I told her to allow him to try. He did and accomplished every part of the task.

We were very fortunate, without exception, throughout Todd's school years to have some of the best teachers and principals who ever taught. The day he left the hospital, even after very long stays, he returned to school. I am sure the teachers were sometimes worried about him. His coughing possibly caused a distraction, but they never made Todd feel different. I thank each teacher today for giving Todd that wonderful gift of normalcy and each student who loved and accepted him for who he was.

JUST A NORMAL KID

We had some narrow escapes through the years. One time, after several days in the hospital, cultures showed our biggest fear had come true. Todd's infection was resistant to all the usual drugs that were on the market. The next day, his doctor learned that a new drug had been approved that week. Todd responded well to the new drug. Once again, we had won a battle against CF.

As National Cystic Fibrosis Foundation Spokesperson, Todd spoke to a group of parents at our state conference. He encouraged them to allow their child to experience life just as they would do if CF were not a factor. Todd believed the CF child would recognize his own limitations. At least let the child try.

He once spoke to one hundred fifty new medical students at UK. He told them not to set limits on a patient just because of a fatal illness. He also believed it was equally important that the child not be given any and everything just because he might die. He believed the child should be disciplined in the same way as their siblings.

Sometimes that can be difficult for a parent to follow. I know. [Todd said that was not true. He said I "beat" him every morning just in case he needed it sometime during the day.] Shortly after being diagnosed with CF, Todd and Angela attended a birthday party. Todd did something he was not supposed to do and I disciplined him. That was before I had heard of time-out. My usual punishment for a serious offense was a paddle on the bottom, so I spanked him.

One of the mothers asked how I could do that when I knew he might die soon. I told her my mind told me that was true, but my heart said he could live to be an adult. If he did, I wanted him to be a contributing member of society, not a spoiled brat.

Now that I am a grandmother, I realize that time-out works just as well or better. I would never spank one of my grandchildren. I probably feel that way just because I have earned the right to spoil and they are *grand*children.

MEETING THE PRESIDENT

Todd enjoyed his high school years. He was a class officer and member and club officer, at one time or another, of most of his school's clubs. He served on the Student Council, acted in the senior play, played on the tennis team, and served as manager for the track team and trainer for the basketball team. He coached Little League and participated in church activities.

He raised the American flag each morning and took it down each afternoon. He later confessed that he enjoyed missing class time to remove the flag at the first sprinkle of rain. When he graduated, Angela took that responsibility. When she graduated, Todd tried to convince Hope to continue the Gibbs tradition. She chose her own path, however, by reading the Bible scripture on the intercom each morning before the school announcements.

The high school years also brought several awards of recognition. The local Jaycees named him "Outstanding Young Person in Allen County." Later, the state Jaycees chose him as "Outstanding Young Kentuckian." The biggest honor came when he was selected "National Cystic Fibrosis Foundation Poster Representative for 1980–81." One of his responsibilities was going to Washington to meet members of Congress and the Senate, Cabinet members, and other heads of federal agencies.

During our visit with the Postmaster General, he gave Todd stamps that were printed for the Winter Olympics. He explained that they were very special because they would not be circulated.

That year the United States did not participate in the Olympics in protest of Russia's invasion of Afghanistan.

The Director of the FBI took Todd to the shooting range and gave us a tour of the FBI building. We met the Attorney General, Benjamin Civilletti, who showed us the long office room where Robert and John Kennedy threw a football to each other to relieve stress when Robert was Attorney General.

We also met the Secretary of Commerce, Secretary of Health and Human Services, Secretary of Transportation, and Secretary of Defense. We were surprised that the office at the Pentagon was larger than The Oval Office.

We were supposed to meet the Secretary of State, but he had resigned that week, so the State Spokesman, Hodding Carter, met with us instead. He gave the daily updates on television regarding the hostage situation. Todd noticed several deflated balloons on his door. Mr. Carter explained he had been so concerned regarding the welfare of our hostages that his staff had sent a balloon representing each hostage. The deflated balloons would stay on his door, regardless of length of time, until the hostages came home. He added, "Todd, I don't think that will be much longer." The following week, the failed rescue attempt occurred. I later wondered if Mr. Carter was thinking of the rescue when he spoke those words.

I could understand the Representatives and Senators taking time to come to the room where we waited. They were having their picture made with Todd to send to the newspapers in their home state. It was good politics. However, the Cabinet Members had nothing to gain by taking time from their busy schedules to meet Todd. Each of them was so nice to our little *country bumpkin* family.

We visited The National Institute of Health and Welfare. They invited Todd to sign the guest register. They told Todd that honor was reserved only for very special guests. They said the next persons given that honor would be the King and Queen of Belgium who were visiting the next week. They later sent us a copy of the guest register page. Above Todd's signature were the

Chancellor, University of Puerto Rico and the Deputy Minister of Health, Hungary, Budapest. Below his name were the signatures of King Baudouin and Queen Fabiola. Between those important signatures was Todd Gibbs, Holland, KY.

Meeting with House Speaker, Tip O'Neil, was a special event. We were not originally scheduled to meet him, but a last minute cancellation in his schedule made it possible. Waiting in the outer office with us was a well-known network news anchor who had an appointment. I was surprised when Mr. O'Neil's assistant told him that his appointment would be delayed, because the Speaker wanted to meet Todd first. We had a long, nice visit, and he gave Todd a pair of gold cufflinks that bore his seal and name. His secretary later told us that Todd should really cherish those, because he gave those only to a select few. I so wish I had those today as a reminder of a very special moment. I hope the person who has those will treasure them.

Many of our appointments lasted longer than the original appointment time, because the dignitaries enjoyed talking to Todd and were impressed by his knowledge of CF and his ability to express the need for research funds. Afterwards, when Todd spoke about it, I reminded him that they probably thought he was much younger than his actual age of fifteen and extremely intelligent for his age.

Our biggest thrill came when we visited the Oval Office to meet President Carter. Our whole family was included. Usually, only the poster child and his parents went to Washington. I asked that the girls be included. Cystic fibrosis affects the siblings as well at the patient. I felt they should enjoy any good resulting from Todd's illness, since they had to suffer through the bad. It was a memorable trip for all of us.

They informed us that Todd could give the President a small, non-monetary gift that represented our state. Kentucky is known for its bluegrass, Kentucky Derby, bourbon, and basketball. We quickly eliminated the first three choices as gifts. Todd loved basketball, especially UK basketball, so he took a Kentucky Wildcat shirt that he asked Kyle Macy to autograph. When the president opened it, he exclaimed, "It's autographed by Kyle Macy," seeming very pleased with his gift.

Todd was surprised that the President of the United States recognized a Kentucky ballplayer. President Carter explained that he enjoyed watching UK basketball, except when they were playing Georgia. He told Todd he would wear the shirt the next time he went jogging.

We had waited in the Oval Office about fifteen minutes before the president's arrival. He was in a cabinet meeting. The next day, he announced that the United States would add more sanctions against Iran. A week later, our forces attempted to rescue the hostages. We were visiting the Oval Office during a very important moment of history. In spite of the pressures of the office, President Carter had taken time to read Todd's biography. He knew many facts about Todd including his being a basketball trainer.

When the President shook my hand, he placed his other hand over mine, looked me directly in my eyes and said, "I'll remember you in my prayers. You have a very special son."

We spent about twenty minutes in the Oval Office with the President. I was almost speechless for one of the few times in my life. I am sure there are many people who would pay to see that. Regardless of one's political persuasion, one cannot help but be awed when thinking of all the historical decisions made in that room. I was standing in the same room where Lincoln had sat!

Our group included a CF foundation director, the foundation's PR director, her assistant, and a Foundation photographer. The PR director almost did not make it through security, because she had a broken leg and was using crutches. As we started to leave, without any prompting, Todd turned toward the President, shook his hand, and thanked him for making the time to meet us.

Surprised by his poise, [as were all of us] President Carter called Todd back to his desk. He said he had something he wanted Todd to have.

When he opened his desk drawer to get and autograph a brochure about the history of The White House, Todd noticed he had several packs of Juicy Fruit gum in his desk drawer. He was most impressed by the worn Bible on the desk. Todd said he could tell it was not for show. It looked well used and worn.

We left with great respect for the man as well as for the office he held. On Todd's sixteenth birthday, the President sent Todd a flag that had hung over the Capitol. He also sent his autographed picture and a very personal letter.

I believe it was on that trip that Todd began his love of politics and the desire to run for office. He admired President Carter, the man. Like him, Todd later taught Sunday school at his Baptist church, became a deacon in that church, and ran for and was elected twice to a political office. That trip was a wonderful memory that resulted from Todd having CF. Todd later referred to such experiences as "gifts" from CF.

TURNING SIXTEEN
WITHOUT HALOS
OR WINGS

When Todd turned sixteen, he earned his driver's license. Although already busy with school activities, he begged to get a part-time job. He became a disc jockey at the local radio station on weekends.

In spite of his already busy schedule and trying to take care of his health, there was one more thing he wanted to do his senior year. He had not tried the band. His friend, Todd Hurt, had been a member throughout school. It sounded like fun to Gibbs. He and Hurt had done almost everything together since first grade. He wanted to try. He had one big problem. He had never learned to play an instrument! Once again, a teacher, band director Sam Kent, went way and beyond his teaching duty to help Todd. He told Todd he could play the cymbals. He attended band camp that summer and practiced and marched during Kentucky's hottest part of the year.

I do not want the reader to picture Todd as a somber, perfect person with a fatal illness who always went about doing good. That was not Todd at all. Anyone who knew Todd will tell you that he was a fun-loving person who loved to laugh. He had a zest for life, and he really lived life. He lived it to the fullest; however, he was definitely *not* perfect. The following letter to the editor illustrates that. The week before, Todd had written in his weekly newspaper column that he was an *angel*. It was his sisters who were bad. The next week, his sister set the record straight with the true story.

NOVEMBER 1, 1990

Letter to the Editor [response from sister regarding last week's Scoop sounds off column]

Dear Editor,
This letter is in response to the October 25, *Scoop sounds off* editorial in which my brother referred to himself as an *angel* while characterizing my sister and me as bad children. I take issue with his inaccurate characterizations, and I would like to set the record straight about my angel—and I use the term loosely—brother.

I begin my case back in October 1972, when my brother received on his eighth birthday a present that will live in infamy in the Gibbs household, a BB gun. I do not know what possessed my parents to purchase such a weapon of destruction for Todd. Just suffice it to say that they quickly lived to regret their decision, as we all did.

After receiving his BB gun, my *angel* brother decided to go bird hunting, as his father had before him, with the family's prized bird dog, Abb. However, Abb was far too valuable a dog to be used in such childish games. Todd, ever resourceful, decided he would have to make do with the next best thing—me! That is why I was forced to act as my brother's personal bird dog!

After placing a tobacco rope around my neck, instructing me on the finer points of pointing birds and informing me I could speak only when spoken to, my *angel* brother and I went hunting. Whenever I spotted a perched bird, [for my brother was not yet skilled at shooting moving objects], I was trained to stop, hike my left leg into the air, and point to the prey with my right arm and index finger extended.

I did this for hours at a time, every afternoon after Todd got home from school, until Christmas! Never mind that I was, and still am, opposed to hunting as a recreational sport.

Never mind that I cried each and every time my brother *bagged* his prey. I did it, because I had no choice.

My *angel* brother had brain washed me into believing that the first-born is automatically entitled to servitude rights over younger siblings. Todd dealt with all signs of rebellion from his sisters swiftly and most effectively. My brother was as successful in crushing early signs of democracy as the Chinese government was in Thiamin Square!

Which explains why, when Todd decided it was time he learned how to shoot moving objects, I did not question his motives when he instructed me to run back and forth across the yard. His point, however, was quickly driven home when Todd carefully took aim, and very deliberately, very cold bloodedly, shot his little sister in the rear end! I, of course, fell to the ground in excruciating pain right underneath our chestnut tree. Hope, who is younger than I and mimicked my every move, also fell down in a very convincing impersonation of her older sister. [Although, she wisely avoided the chestnut tree and their prickly briars.]

As I struggled to my feet, picking chestnut briars from my hands, arms, and feet, and gingerly rubbing my bruised posterior, my *angel* brother was laughing uncontrollably! He assumed since Hope was acting as if she had also been shot, that he had been able to "shoot two sisters with one BB."

Todd's little bottom hurt, too, after I tattled on him. Just as it did about four months later when Mom discovered he and a friend had been shooting out the windows in the *non-essential* rooms of the house. To this day, I still believe he got off easy. [I was campaigning for capital punishment and the permanent confiscation of the BB gun.]

Let me assure you, ladies and gentlemen of the jury, that the BB Gun incident is just a chapter out of my brother's *angelic* life. I could tell you stories that would make child psychologists cringe. Todd was not an *angel,* unless, of course, he was referring to the fallen one.

I rest my case.

By Angela Gibbs [sister of Todd]

Todd's youth pastor, Ken Goforth, shares in his tribute other examples of Todd's "not so perfect" behavior. When I learned about the cymbal incident, I was horrified. Todd said, "But, Mom, I didn't do it to be mean. I was just having fun." I do not know how the band director reacted. I just know what I did.

Todd became a member of the pep, concert, and marching bands, and began a close and life-long friendship with Sam. Even as an adult, he stayed involved with the band's activities. When the band marched in a parade in PA, Todd went along to take pictures for the local newspaper and serve as a chaperone. He marched along side the band the entire route.

At graduation, Todd received the speech award and "Outstanding Student in School and Community" award. He was listed in Who's Who in America's High Schools. He had been on numerous television shows, and interviewed by newspaper reporters. They wrote how he had achieved so much in spite of CF. Sometimes, I believe Todd did it *because* of CF. He realized that he did not have time to waste.

GROWING UP

Since Todd could drive himself and had such an independent nature, he began going alone to Lexington for his check-ups. I had completed my college degree and was teaching English at the local high school.

Dr. Wilson had left the CF clinic, and Dr. Jamshed Kanga had become Todd's CF doctor. He felt immediate confidence in Dr. Kanga's skills.

I no longer stayed with Todd when he was hospitalized. I came to realize that it was easier sleeping on the floor beside his bed than worrying about his health one hundred sixty miles away. Todd was an adult and could tell me only what he wanted me to know. He had always pretended that he was not as sick as everyone else thought he was. He even convinced me many times.

I am sure every parent feels pride when a child graduates. I did when my girls graduated. There is a different emotion, however, when your child has a fatal illness. It was something doctors had told us we would probably never see. Not only had he lived to graduate, he had lived those years to the fullest.

As I watched Todd walk on stage to receive his diploma, I remembered my feelings at his sixth grade graduation ceremony. I had been emotional, fearing that would be the only time I would see Todd in a cap and gown walking across the stage to receive a diploma. At his high school graduation, I did not realize I would later see him graduate from college.

During one of our serious talks, [or what I was trying to make serious] I told Todd if I made a list of the top ten persons, living or dead, whom I most admired, he would be on that list. I explained that I admired him because he had never used CF as an excuse. He said, "Well, Mama, that's not quite true. There was the time in second grade..."

Todd Hurt and Todd Gibbs had done something that warranted Mrs. Woodward's most severe punishment, a spanking. [Neither Todd nor Mrs. Woodward remembered later what the offense had been, but Todd was sure she was in the wrong!] She took the boys outside the classroom into the hall. Before she delivered the punishment, she asked if a spanking could hurt Gibbs's cystic fibrosis or Hurt's hemophilia. Todd said, "Now Mama, what is a seven-year-old going to say?" Both boys answered yes, and they escaped the paddling. Later Hurt's dad learned about the incident and told Mrs. Woodward to "lay it on" whenever necessary. Todd's grandmother, who taught first grade in the building with Sharon, soon learned how Gibbs had responded and "upset his apple cart."

She told Mrs. Woodward that, in fact, she had paddled Gibbs the year before. [Todd's only major punishment his entire school years.] She had caught the two Todds trying to look in the window of the girls' bathroom. As an adult, Todd declared it was an unfair punishment. Unlike the taller Hurt, because of Gibbs's small stature, he had been unable to see a thing!

AN EMPTY ROOM

As I stood at the door to Todd's empty room, I felt conflicting emotions. Probably every parent who has a child with a fatal disease has contemplated how he or she could face life when his or her child is no longer at home. I know I had. Todd took pride in decorating his room in a patriotic theme and kept it spotless. Now, that room was empty!

I was close to crying, but they were tears of both sadness and joy. I had always assumed that when I faced Todd's empty room, it would be because of his death. Although my heart had dreamed of a long future for Todd, my brain said he would be unable to have a full time job and his own apartment. My heart's dream had become a reality.

As any other mother who watches her first-born leave the nest, there were some tears of sadness. I was really going to miss Todd's presence in our home; however, most of my tears were the result of joy. I could still see my son and watch as he grew into his adult life. That was something special.

Todd and I had so much fun together, painting, buying furniture, and preparing for his independent life. He took pride in the decorating, and as he had with his room at home, he kept it spotless. If there was one thing Todd failed to experience in life, it was the messy bachelor life.

Todd was working as a disc jockey at the radio station where he had been working part-time for two years. Soon, he became the News Director. It was not long until he obtained the nickname "Scoop," because people said that he was always the first to know and deliver the news to the community. After his on-air hours, he spent many more collecting the news. He did not want to repeat the same news throughout the day. He wanted his listeners to know that if something happened in our little community, they could turn on the radio and get the facts from him.

He rode with the police to drug busts. He went to every fire unless he was on-air. He went to the City-County building regularly to gather news. A street was even named for him, Scoop Boulevard. When I teased him that it went to the city dump, he reminded me that it was the thought that counted, then laughed. During this period, in spite of his "full-force-ahead" lifestyle, Todd's health continued to improve. He was hospitalized once or twice a year, usually for what he called, "a routine clean-up."

After three months of paying rent, Todd, at the age of eighteen, decided paying rent was a waste. He wanted to invest his money in a home. He obtained a loan with the Federal Housing Administration and moved into a new brick home in a new subdivision that was under construction.

From that point until his death, Todd always had some type of home improvement project. He was always adding some type of shrub, tree, or flower. We painted and papered. He built a deck with his father's help. If he could not add something new, he did what I had always done. He rearranged all the furniture.

He became the emcee for many community and school events. He did play-by-play of basketball games for the radio station. He began writing a weekly newspaper column called "Scoop sounds off" for the local newspaper. He took his sound system to the schools for various events. In fact, the day that two of his closest CF friends died, he had promised to work the sound system for graduation that night. Todd did as he had promised. I did not realize until later how difficult that was for him.

As a child and teenager, Todd embraced as many activities as possible. He had so many things he wanted to do and knew he had a short time in which to do them. After graduation, he looked for new opportunities, so he could contribute to his church and community.

LaRecea Gibbs

From 1983 until his death in 1995, Todd was a member, at one time or another, of eight community boards. He especially enjoyed his seven years serving with the Young Woman of the Year Board. [Formerly known as Junior Miss] He was planning to be a judge or emcee for three of the contests the summer he was placed on the transplant list. He stayed busy in spite of having a fatal disease.

The minister stated at Todd's funeral that he did more living in thirty-one years than most of us do in seventy. Donald and I had chosen quality over quantity when he was diagnosed. We thought it was an either-or decision. In the end, Todd achieved both quality and quantity. Even though the quantity was short compared to the average lifespan, it was a life fully lived and enjoyed.

I believe one of the reasons he was able to live such an abundant life is because of our community. Scottsville is the only county seat in Allen County, KY. It is a small, rural town. Sometimes it seems everyone knows each other, their uncles and aunts, their successes and failures.

The community embraced Todd and appreciated and recognized his accomplishments. The Woman's Club recognized him as their "Citizen of the Year" and the Jaycees gave them their highest honor, "Allen County Citizen of the Year." During his acceptance speech, Todd stated that a girlfriend had complained once that he did too much for the community. He needed to learn to say "'No." Todd had replied that it was difficult to say "No" to the community that had always said "Yes" to him. He stated that the community had always been there to support and encourage him. They had laughed with him, cried with him, and given him advice. Sometimes the advice came when he was refereeing a ballgame, he laughingly added. I sometimes wonder if Todd's life would have been as full if he had been born and lived in a different place.

Needing to supplement his income, Todd started his own business. He called it Scoop Sounds. He added to his sound system and collected a wide variety of music. He became the disc jockey for many school dances, weddings, reunions, etc. Todd needed to supplement his income, because he wanted to be financially independent. We were told when Todd was young that he qualified for Social Security Supplemental Income. Whether from pride or stupidity, [we thought then it was pride, but after financial difficulties, I realize it was probably just stupidity] we did not apply. When Todd became independent, and no longer covered under our insurance, he went to apply for Medicare.

The social security representative told him that he could also receive disability, which included a monthly stipend, a housing allotment and food stamps, *if and only if,* he quit his job and stayed home. Todd refused the offer. I remember our walking to the car together, tears streaming down his face. Todd said, "Mom, I'd rather be dead than to sit on my butt!"

That was typical of Todd's attitude toward life. He never looked for the easy road. He accepted the Medicare but declined the other benefits. When he was elected to the city council, he became part of their insurance plan, no longer needing Medicare.

Todd was in the hospital on his eighteenth birthday, a big milestone year. I remember walking toward the car after celebrating with him and feeling, "This stinks. To be in the hospital on such an important day just isn't fair." Then I remembered we never expected Todd to be alive at eighteen and said a silent prayer of gratitude. He would also be in the hospital on his twenty-first, thirtieth, and thirtieth-first.

When Todd was diagnosed, I searched for books that would help me understand what we were facing. I wanted more than just the medical facts. I wanted something that would give a family's viewpoint. One day, on my way to class at the university, I took a wrong turn and ended up on a street that I had never taken. Trying to look at the street signs, I was distracted by a sign that said Christian Bookstore. How ironic. I thought I had been to every bookstore in the area. I went in, explained what I wanted, expecting the usual answer. I was surprised when the manager said they had received a new shipment that day which was still boxed. She thought she had ordered a book by the mother of a child who had cystic fibrosis. If I would wait, she would be happy to look.

She returned with the book, *If I Die at Thirty.* I thought it was a wonderful coincidence. Later, I came to believe that God had directed me to that store. That was the first of many times that God provided the answer, sometimes before I even asked the question. At the time, having just been told Todd would not live past twelve, I thought if I could have thirty years with Todd—what a gift! Of course, thirty years was not enough.

When researchers discovered the gene causing CF in 1990, Todd decided to attend college. He enrolled in the fall, 1991, seeking a major in the field of Television and Broadcasting and a minor in Government. When he graduated from high school, the average life expectancy for CF was eighteen. He was afraid if he went to college to peruse a degree at that time, he might die before he had the chance to work in his chosen field. By remaining at the radio station, he could experience, on a small scale, what he wanted to do on a larger basis. He often laughed and said he wanted Peter Jennings's job! Well, actually, I am not sure that he was kidding. *[The following excerpt from his weekly newspaper column explains what that discovery meant to Todd.]*

SCOOP SOUNDS OFF

DISCOVERY OF THE
CYSTIC FIBROSIS GENE

I was at home Thursday night when my friend, Donnie Meador, called me. He said he heard on ABC radio that scientists had corrected the defective cystic fibrosis gene and were hoping for a cure in the next few years. Instead of being optimistic, I was pessimistic. "I think you misunderstood the report," I told Donnie. It had only been one year since researchers had discovered which gene was defective in cystic fibrosis patients, so it was impossible that the defective gene had been corrected. Researchers said it would take years to correct the gene that causes this disease, which is the number one genetic killer of children and young adults. The news was just too good too soon. Well, I was wrong. It was true.

The incredible news came the day I was set to travel to Lexington for a CF fund raising event and spend a day with my doctor, Jamshed Kanga. The news of the latest medical breakthrough left him, and everyone else at the University of Kentucky who have been fighting this disease, with new hope and optimism. Every time researchers make a new breakthrough, everyone at UK sees it as a victory, no matter how small the new discovery may be. And this is no small discovery. This is *big!*

During my lifetime, I've had hundreds of doctors, nurses, and respiratory therapists. They are more than just the people that take care of me when I'm sick. They are my friends and the battle against CF is just as real for them as it is for me. Most of them know what it's like to lose someone they cared about to this disease. They have watched some of us grow up, and they have watched some of us die. But their battle against this disease continues, and the latest breakthrough is an extra incentive to keep on fighting.

Over the years, some of my most special friendships have started at the A.B. Chandler Medical Center at the University of Kentucky. Over the weekend, I visited one of my respiratory therapists, LaDawn. Our friendship started while she was *beating on me* as part of the treatment to loosen the mucus in my lungs. There have been times we sat and watched the Wildcats play basketball on television while she "hit my back" for what seemed like hours. We've been to Florida to visit friends together, and we've been to funerals to say goodbye to friends together. But our friendship started at UK. LaDawn is just one of hundreds of respiratory therapists who has spent hours and hours trying to keep my lungs clear. They seem to be doing a good job.

Then there are the nurses. It's easy to get close to them, because they are the ones directly involved in the patient's care. They spend hours taking notes, starting IV's, [not always on the first try] taking vital signs, giving medicine and just talking. There have been some nurses that just did their job and left. But most UK nurses are special. They have taken me out to dinner, since hospital food isn't the best. They have taken me out to movies, since hospital television isn't much better. They have visited me in Scottsville, and I've gone as far as Alaska to see them. They are special people with a special purpose.

Then there have been the doctors, and there have been hundreds. But of all my doctors, two special ones come to mind, Dr. David Wilson and Dr. Jamshed Kanga. Dr. Wilson was my doctor for more than eight years at UK. He was always the one you turned to for wisdom and strength at times you needed it the most. He was the typical looking doctor, white-headed with a white coat. But he wasn't your typical doctor. He was a teaching doctor, and even though I was never one of his students, I learned a lot from him. He's still at UK teaching future doctors how to cure diseases such as CF, but his fight with CF is over. [Dr. Wilson is currently Professor of Pediatrics, Dean, University of Kansas School of Medicine]

The new fighter is Jamshed Kanga. He's not your typical looking doctor. He looks more like the guy that wakes you at three o'clock a.m. to take your blood. But there are few smarter doctors than Kanga. My relationship with Kanga is not your average doctor-patient relationship. He's my friend. We have spent hours talking about everything you can imagine. He's given me advice, even when I didn't ask for it. And I've given him advice, because he needed it. We've argued about how long I was going to stay in the hospital or what the nurse and I were going to do while we were out of the hospital on pass. At times, it's been hard to determine if he was my doctor or my father. I've made medical rounds with him, and once he let me sign his name to my hospital discharge papers. No one ever knew, until now. He's not your average doctor, but UK is not your average hospital.

UK has always been the place I went when everyone else failed. After being hospitalized for three weeks, a doctor once told me I had a week to live. The next day I went to UK by ambulance, and, two weeks later, I walked out of the medical center on my own. That was eight years ago. I'm glad that doctor was wrong, and I'm glad UK was there.

A lot has happened at UK, but the main thing has been the fight to beat CF. The doctors, nurses, respiratory therapists, and everyone else involved have committed themselves to fight a disease they cannot defeat. But now, all that has changed. Everyone can now see the light at the end of the tunnel, and now they know this fight is winnable. It may not be tomorrow, or next month, or even next year, but now we all know a cure is in sight. Slowly the dream is becoming a reality.

THE BEGINNING
OF COLLEGE

After the gene discovery, Todd enrolled in college as a full-time student. For the first time, since learning of D.K.'s death, Todd believed he could possibly live a long life, so he decided to prepare for that life by earning a college degree.

I was concerned that Todd would miss the social side of college. He would be commuting the twenty-five miles from his home to the campus instead of living on campus. He planned to continue working at the bank, keep referring ball games, serving as city councilman, his church activities, his weekly newspaper column, plus his community and civic responsibilities of serving on several boards. I did not understand how he maintained his already busy schedule. How could he possibly add a social life as a college student? As usual, Todd surprised me, and instead of cutting back his activities, he just added more.

After his first semester, I asked him what he found most surprising about college life. I questioned if he had more respect for his mama's degrees now that he was a student himself and understood how difficult college could be. Hoping for one of those Hallmark moments where my son would express his great admiration for me, instead he answered, "Not really, Mom. You've just gone to college all your life. Let me see ... since you began college, we won World War II, developed an atomic bomb, sent a man to the moon ..." I reminded him I was born during the war, and shortly before the bomb, but had to admit I was in college for the moon landing. Then Todd became serious and said he was most surprised by the students themselves. He was not having difficulty with the classes but said, "Mom, some of the students are just weird. Many don't even know why they are attending college. They're just there." I reminded him that he was far more mature than most persons his age, probably because of his life experiences.

Soon, Todd became very involved in college activities and began making new friends just as he always had. His sister, Hope, was also a student at Western. Both were pursuing degrees in Broadcasting and had several classes together. Their college years strengthened their already close relationship. Hope was a member of a sorority, so she introduced Todd to her sorority sisters. Todd became close friends to some of them. When Hope moved into the sorority house, Todd visited often, sometimes baking cupcakes for the house or other favors and goodies. Was he visiting only because of his love for his sister? I doubt it. Todd was no dummy. He liked girls, and that house was full of beautiful girls! Later, the sorority honored him by naming him their "King of Diamonds." Todd was thrilled.

Todd also became friends with two former presidents of Western, Dr. Dero Downing, and Dr. Kelly Thompson as well as then Western's president, Dr. Thomas Meredith. Those relationships enriched his college years. I knew they made a positive impact on Todd's life. After I read Dr. Downing's tribute for this book, I realized the effect had been mutual.

TODD ADDS
ANOTHER JOB

Todd added an additional job. He began working with Jeff Younglove in Western's Public Relations department with his primary focus on special events. Todd really enjoyed its challenges and rewards. He worked with the basketball games and helped organize and promote concerts. He enjoyed working with famous country singers when they did a concert at Western. He was especially impressed with Vince Gill. He said most of the stars remained on their bus until concert time. Vince had come inside and played a basketball game with some of the student volunteers until time for the concert. After the concert, Todd was escorting Vince to his bus through a private entrance. It was Todd's responsibility to help the star avoid a rush of fans and get to the bus without incident. Many of the student volunteers were standing in the hall just hoping to get a glimpse of Vince as he passed. Instead, he stopped and did not go to his bus until every fan had the opportunity to meet him and receive his autograph. That incident gave Todd great respect for the country star.

In addition to his already hectic work schedule, he began working at Western's public radio station. There is where he met and fell in love with his future bride who also worked there in the news department.

CYSTIC FIBROSIS
REARS ITS UGLY HEAD

Cystic fibrosis did not forget it was a part of Todd's life even though he tried to make it a minor part. The second week of his first semester of college, Todd became very ill from complications of the flu and had to be hospitalized. Since he was so ill, I used my sick days as a high school teacher to stay in Lexington with him.

I was lying on the floor next to Todd's bed when late one night he called, "Mom, are you awake?" I had actually dozed off, but of course, I answered that I was awake. Todd asked, "Mom, will you do something for me?" I thought he probably wanted a Baskin Robbins run. During past hospitalizations, I often went, sometimes late at night, getting ice cream for nurses and roommates, as well as Todd. I answered that of course I would. I had no idea he was thinking of the future or the difficulty of his request.

Todd asked if I would speak at his funeral. After a difficult silence on my part, I asked him what he wanted me to say. He said that he wanted me to thank everyone for always being there for him. In spite of all his hospitalizations, his community and friends always sent cards, flowers, and gifts. They had never forgotten him.

Sensing I was getting close to tears, Todd said. "Mom, you'll know what to say. I'm not worried about that. I'm just worried you won't know when to shut up!" Of course, that eased the tension and I had to laugh. Through the years, Todd often mentioned things he wanted at his funeral. It was never with sadness or remorse, but as casually as if he was scheduling a class or planning a camping trip.

Two years later, I conducted an interview with him for a class assignment. I was pursuing a Rank I in education. In Kentucky, a Rank III is earned when a teacher receives his/her Bachelor's degree. With thirty more hours, a person receives a Master's degree and considered a Rank II. I was studying for my Rank I, which is thirty more hours, giving me certification to become a guidance counselor. Todd often teased me that it took me eighteen years to get my Bachelor's, ten years to earn my Master's, and since I was completing my Rank I in eighteen months, he felt I was finally "getting the hang of this school thing" and should go for my doctorate.

The video was to be a ten to fifteen minute counseling session showing the skills I had learned. Todd agreed to portray my client. We became so involved in the session that it lasted over an hour. I learned a lot about his feelings during that session.

It was only during that interview that I learned how very sick he had been when he had the flu. I asked him if he was scared with each hospitalization, afraid it might be the one that would not respond to the antibiotics. He answered that out of eighty-two hospitalizations, there were only two when he felt he would not leave the hospital. One of those was when he was hospitalized from complications of the flu. [Todd had once asked to see his hospitalization charts when he was bored and needed something to do. That is how he knew the number.] The other instance was when a doctor told him she had done all she could, and he probably would not live longer than a week.

He stated that usually he could tell a couple weeks before a hospitalization that he was getting sick. The complications from the flu came suddenly, and he did not remember the first few days. He remembered waking one night and could not get a breath. It was at that time he thought he would never leave the hospital. That was when he asked me to speak at his funeral.

I told him about a time when doctors thought he could not survive. Didn't he see how worried I was? He said he did not care what I thought, his sisters, dad, friends, or even the doctors thought. He said we might think we know, and he might not be able to raise his head from the pillow, but he knew he was still in control. It was only when he became concerned that he began to worry.

Through the years, Todd and I talked a lot about CF and his feelings toward it. It often came without warning, and if he saw I was becoming emotional, he would crack a joke. I often ended up laughing instead of crying. He talked about organ donation, selection for pallbearer, and choosing donations instead of flowers.

One time, he announced he wanted his casket placed in center court of the basketball gymnasium for his funeral. He said some of his happiest moments were associated with basketball, then joked, "Besides, I've always wanted to see the gym full once." He added that Danny Tabor who had given him his first job, owner and play-by-play radio announcer for all the high school games, could sell advertising spots and they could broadcast the funeral. They could then donate the ad money to CF. I knew Todd was joking and trying to relieve the tension of talking about the possible future.

On another occasion, he stated that he wanted Coach Young to speak at his funeral, instead of a minister. He did not want a "valley of the shadow of death" type funeral. He wanted it to be a celebration. I said that having his funeral in a gym with a coach speaking would make people think he did not believe in God, only basketball. He answered, "Mom, who knows me better than Coach Young? Besides, if I haven't shown people that I'm a Christian while I'm living, I think it's a little late to try at my funeral."

TODD THE PROTECTOR

While preparing to write the following chapters, I watched the video repeatedly. We were discussing some serious subjects, but as I watched, it was easy to see the special bond Todd and I shared. I recognized that both Todd and I used humor as a self-defense when discussing serious or difficult topics. I told him that when he was a child and teenager, he had discussed everything about CF with me. Now that he was in his twenties, he no longer talked with me about his concerns or fears. Both Dr. Kanga and LaDawn had told me that Todd was trying to protect me.

I said. "Todd, it's almost like you've become the parent, and I've become the child." He answered, "Well, Mom, you need someone to parent you. You sure aren't doing too good yourself." Then, he became serious and said, "Mom, just as you want to protect *me* from CF, I want to protect *you* from CF." He added that since becoming an adult, he had discussed his feelings about cystic fibrosis with only two persons, Dr. Kanga and Jack, his CF friend about whom Todd wrote in his journal. In a sense, Todd had become the protector of our family. Even before Todd's father and I divorced when he was eighteen, it was often Todd to whom the girls turned for advice and help. They knew he would take care of them and protect them. Wise beyond his years, I also trusted his advice and asked his opinion.

Several months after my car wreck, I became depressed. I was in constant pain from the nerve damage in my arm and even after thirty hours of surgery, I was unable to move my fingers, hand, or any part of my left arm. I was especially sad that I could no longer teach. Once, when Todd came by to check on me, he explained that I was lucky just to be alive. Doctors had been uncertain if I would live.

Then he asked, "Mom, do you know why you lived?" I expected him to say it was because of his many prayers or that it would be difficult for him to live without me. Instead, when I asked why, he said, "Heaven wouldn't have you, and hell was afraid you'd take over." As usual, Todd made me laugh through my tears.

Regardless of the seriousness of the situation or topic, Todd could always make me laugh. I admired his faith, courage, independence, work ethic, and his love and loyalty for his family and friends. However, it is that sense of humor and his laugh that I still miss the most.

In the video, I told him it was almost superhuman the way he lived in spite of CF. I asked did he not sometimes question why he had CF and he answered, "No." He explained that he did not think God said, "Okay, I am going to give Todd Gibbs cystic fibrosis, Todd Hurt hemophilia, Angela Gibbs asthma, and make Hope Gibbs okay. I do not think God works that way. I do believe he has a plan for my life. At twenty-six, I still do not know what it is, but why do people always need to know the answer to why? Some things just are. I do not understand when Christians doubt God when something bad happens to them or God does not answer their prayer the way they want. If God answered every prayer, 'Yes' the way people expect, then we would have heaven on earth. There would be no need for faith. That is where faith comes in. I just accept I have CF. I do not need to ask why."

He continued that he sometimes got mad at CF when he had to be hospitalized and put his life on hold or something happened like Jack and Melissa dying, but everyone was entitled to a few days to be sad and grieve. Whenever anyone faced an obstacle, it was okay to be down for a few days, but then you just had to get off your butt and go forward again.

Todd and I had a special mother-son relationship. In the video, Todd said he thought one reason was a positive result of his having cystic fibrosis. "When you spend weeks in a hospital room with someone, you either grow to love them more or begin to hate them. Now, [he added with that special laugh] there were a couple of instances where I came close to the hate, and I'm sure you did too, but it made our relationship closer."

When Todd applied for college, he did not realize what a life-changing experience it would be. He not only earned his degree, he met his future bride.

Todd had several past relationships, but I knew, almost from the start, that he felt differently about Sarah. At Todd's commencement, she was one of two persons who read each graduate's name as the graduates walked across the stage to receive their degree. Dr. Kanga and his family and I were sitting together. I am not sure which one of us felt the most pride. He stated, "Now that we have Todd graduating from college, it is time to find him a wife." I think he was kidding, but I told him that he might be looking at her. Sarah and Todd had just begun dating.

Seven months later, which Todd described as the happiest day of his life, he and Sarah married. The ceremony was performed in Todd's church with a background of Christmas trees and Christmas decorations.

I was happy for Todd. I had thirty years of memory making with him as a son, now it was time for him to make memories as a husband.

THE BEGINNING
OF THE END

Up to this point, I have enjoyed reliving my journey with Todd. I have smiled and laughed to myself as I recalled the memories and remembered the joy Todd brought into my life. Now, for the first time, I can understand what authors mean when they refer to writer's block. Perhaps, it is because I am beginning to write about the end—the end of Todd's journey.

Soon after his marriage, Todd's health began to decline. He was hospitalized the Easter following his wedding. In May, Todd returned to Lexington for his check-up. Before going home, he came by to see me at work. He never interrupted me when I was working, so I knew he was very upset. He said that his CF had worsened, and Dr. Kanga had told him it was time to consider a lung transplant.

Almost in tears, he asked, "Mom, how am I ever going to tell Sarah? She didn't sign up for this." At that point, he was most concerned about her feelings and not his. The following month, on Father's day, Todd was admitted to the hospital. The decision regarding a transplant had to be made.

It is difficult to describe the almost four months of hospitalizations and waiting. It is the last miles of a thirty-one year journey with my son. Todd's daily journal entries reflect it during that period far better than I can possibly do. I was there with him a majority of the time; however, it was not until I read his journal, the year after he died, that I really saw it from Todd's perspective.

When Todd was placed on the transplant list, I quit my job in order to stay with him during the week. Since I was no longer teaching, mine was just a job, not a career, even though I was actually making more money than when I taught.

Sarah would keep working and stay with him on weekends. After he received his lungs, he would need to live in Lexington for six months to be close to the transplant doctors, so she was saving her time off for after the transplant. Todd's friends, Roddy and Melissa, had invited them to stay at their home.

Todd often spoke about how difficult it was only having Sarah's presence on weekends. He told me I was doing a great job, and he appreciated everything I was doing, but the weekdays seemed so long and the weekends so short without her presence. They were married only ten months. Four of those, he spent in the hospital.

I am so glad I had that time with Todd in the hospital while he was waiting for the transplant. I did not realize then what a great gift it truly was. Those days, weeks, and months together at the end have given me some wonderful, as well as heart-breaking, memories.

I have never known anyone who fought harder to live than he did those last months. Todd suffered terribly, but he never complained. He was determined to beat CF, and he intended to endure whatever it took until he received his transplant. Although he had been very sick before and hospitalized many times, I had never seen him in such intense pain. There were days during those last weeks when it was almost unbearable for me to watch him and to feel so helpless to give him any relief. I watched him struggle to type daily entries into his journal in spite of his arms shaking so badly it was difficult for him to hit the correct keys. He continued writing because, as he explained to me, it was important to him to tell his story. He never stopped trying to have a positive impact on others or share his joy of life and the lessons he had learned from living with CF.

Even while waiting for a transplant, Todd continued trying to make a difference. He wrote the letter about the importance of organ donation and sent it to several newspapers across the state. He was so pleased to learn that it resulted in a large increase of organ donors. Two televisions stations went to the hospital to do interviews about organ donation and his unique approach to living. The last interview he gave was just three weeks before his death. CBS Network was doing a national segment during the week of Thanksgiving about the relationship between prayer and the healing process. Todd and Dr. Kanga gave interviews as part of that segment. Sadly, Todd was not alive when it aired to know if his words had an impact.

I fear I failed Todd while he was waiting for his transplant when he needed me the most. When he would ask, "What if I don't get my lungs in time, Mama?" instead of listening to the fears he might have, I would say, "Oh, Todd, I'm sure they will come in time. You have an amazing life ahead."

I had listened in the past when Todd talked about difficult topics, things he wanted when he died or his feelings about CF, in spite of the difficulty. I did not listen, as I now wish I had, in the end. I thought I needed to remain positive and strong for Todd. I did not want him to think that I was feeling anything but positive thoughts regarding the transplant. Now, I question if I actually believed that strongly that he would receive the lungs or was I just in denial?

When I read his journal entries, I am haunted by the fear that I may have disappointed him when he needed me most. I was there for him physically. Was I there for him emotionally?

Throughout Todd's life, I tried to do everything I possibly could for him. I knew from experience that the most difficult part of grief is not what one did for a person who died, but what one failed to do, not what one said, but what one left unsaid. I thought I would not have any of those regrets, because I often told him how I loved and admired him, and had tried hard to make CF a little more bearable. Now, I sometimes feel guilty regarding those last months.

We all thought that Todd would receive his transplant and he would be able to begin a new life, one without the complications of CF. When I *did* have doubts, I kept those thoughts to myself.

About two weeks before his death, I realized that Todd's condition was declining swiftly and feared and came to believe he would not get his new lungs in time to save his life.

For years, my heart and mind did battle when I thought of Todd's future. [If Todd could hear me say that, he would respond that I never had a good mind, and after two open-heart surgeries, my heart is not much better.] This time my heart agreed with what my mind had always tried to get me to face.

I would return home on weekends telling friends how very sick he was. Sarah and my daughters saw a different Todd when they visited on weekends. I realize now that Todd was using all his energy to hide the severity of his illness from them, trying to protect them as he had done years earlier with me.

About ten days before his death, even though I knew I would not get to spend as much time with Todd, I suggested to Sarah that she take some time off work to stay with him. I feared she would not need the time she was saving for after his transplant. I knew how much her presence meant to him. She did.

The day Todd went to the ICU for the last time, the room was filled with family and friends. We were in the sitting area joining his room. His pastor, Dr. Price, led us in prayer as we all held hands. I do not remember a lot about that morning, but I do remember his saying, "God, you understand what LaRecea is feeling, because you watched your son die on the cross." Those words were very special to me, because I had not thought of it like that.

Later, I went into his room to talk to Todd. We knew he would not be able to speak to us after they put him on the respirator. I cannot remember what I said to him or what he said to me. After years of remembering exact conversations with Todd, why can I not remember those special last moments and words?

LaRecea Gibbs

THE FINAL STEPS OF TODD'S JOURNEY

On October 11, doctors put Todd in the ICU and placed him on a respirator. I only slept three hours from that point until Todd's death on the thirteenth. I did not want to miss a single precious moment that I could be with him. The hospital allowed two persons to stay with Todd at all times, except during shift changes. Sarah stayed with him during the day while my family and I waited in the ICU lobby. She left the hospital each night around eight to spend the night at the Parsons, so that time became very special to us. That is when we were able to be with Todd. Since Todd's last admission, he had been staying in Happy's room. It was actually a suite, the regular patient room with a sitting room beside it. It was named after former Kentucky governor, Happy Chandler, who stayed in that suite whenever he was hospitalized. The hospital, A.B. Chandler Medical Center was also named in his honor. It made Todd's long hospital stay much easier for us. The hospital saved the room for Todd when he was sent to the ICU. The family could use the room to rest if we desired.

Around midnight, the morning of the thirteenth, Angela insisted I get some rest. She would stay with Todd. Around three, we switched places. Like me, she had been unable to sleep.

Todd was having a difficult night. Even though sedated, he was very restless. It was easy to see that he was still in great pain. His hands were tied so he could not pull on the ventilator. That was very difficult to watch. A man who had always been so active was unable to move.

Before leaving his room, Angela asked the nurse if anything else could be done to ease his pain. She answered that yes, she had orders for a stronger medication. Later, when I went into his room, the medication had taken effect. The nurse had bathed and shaved him and untied his hands. He was resting more comfortably than I had seen in a long time.

As I was sitting beside Todd's bed, the thought came to me, "This is the day I lose my son." However, I expected it to be later in the afternoon or evening. I sat on Todd's bed and told him it was okay for him to crossover. I thanked him for all the joy he had brought into my life and all the lessons he had taught me. I promised him I would remember those lessons and that I would be okay. I also promised I would enjoy life and laugh again, just as he had taught me by his example. I said I would take time to look at each rainbow and think of him.

I have heard that hearing is the last sense to go. I believe and hope Todd heard me. Weeks after his death, I learned that Angela had shared a similar moment just before she left his room and had read him the twenty-third Psalms.

About thirty minutes after I talked to Todd, the nurse came to check his vitals. I am still unsure how I sensed that something was terribly wrong. The nurse did not indicate that his condition had worsened, but I explained that his sister, grandmother, and best friend were upstairs resting. "Should I get them?" He answered, "Yes."

When we returned to the ICU waiting room, a nurse met us. She said Todd had gone into cardiac arrest and doctors were trying to resuscitate him. I asked if I could go in just to say goodbye. I promised I would not do anything that would interfere. I had watched enough medical shows to realize the answer was probably no. The nurse said she would ask.

She quickly returned and told me to follow her. When I entered Todd's room, he was surrounded by doctors and nurses, some performing CPR, while others injected his IV with some type of medicine. I touched his hand, quickly told him goodbye and that I loved him. As I started to leave, a doctor put his arm around me and said I should stay. He guided me to the head of Todd's bed.

Angela had gone to càll Sarah and learned she had just left the Parsons and was on her way to the hospital. I asked the doctor if Angela could come into the room, which they allowed.

When doctors pronounced Todd dead, I experienced a feeling entirely unexpected. I expected to feel the gut-wrenching agony and pain that I felt. I did not expect to, also, feel a type of peace. I could almost hear Todd saying, as he crossed over, "Why did I fight so hard to live?"

Angela left to await Sarah's arrival. She did not know Todd had died. Hope, who had been resting at a friend's home nearby was already at the hospital. After Sarah and her parents spent time alone with Todd, everyone, except me, went to Todd's room to pack. Since he had been in the hospital for three months straight, it would be a long, difficult task. I expected the staff to quickly remove Todd's body so they could clean the room for another patient. I was forgetting it was the UK Medical Center, and like Todd had often said, the best hospital anywhere. They told me to stay as long as I wanted.

I do not know if it was their usual policy or if an unusually compassionate staff was on duty that morning. I do know that they not only did everything possible to save Todd's life, they gave me the greatest gift possible—that special time alone with my son to grieve my loss. I am forever grateful to each of them.

They allowed me to remove his IV, other tubes, and help remove the ventilator. I knew he hated all the tubes and had feared being on the ventilator, and it made me feel like I was setting him free. That may seem strange to most people. If someone had told me they had done that with a loved one, I would probably think it odd, but that gave me some measure of peace that I still cannot explain or describe.

Todd had never worn hospital clothes except for the previous few days. When he was young, his grandmother often made unusual and fun pajamas for him to wear. One time, she used embroidery to enhance a pair. As he became a teenager, he always wore sweats or casual clothing. I could not tolerate the thought of his returning home in a hospital gown. I asked his nurse and his respiratory therapist if they would help me dress him in something else. They offered to do the dressing themselves, but I wanted to do it. It would be the last thing I could ever do for Todd.

For his birthday, his sisters and I had given him hospital clothing. The girls gave him casual bottoms and I had a t-shirt printed with one of his favorite quotes, "The human spirit and prayer are more powerful than any drug." I dressed him in those clothes.

Todd requested that quote be placed over his bed after his transplant. He wanted everyone to know a higher power was really in control of his recovery. A friend, Kim Marsh, had cross-stitched the quote for his birthday. Instead of it being over his hospital bed, it was near his casket.

Soon, word spread throughout the hospital of Todd's passing. Because of his many hospitalizations, many of the staff, nurses, doctors, therapists, cleaning staff, kitchen staff, and all people whom Todd had touched through his numerous hospitalizations, came to pay their respects and say goodbye. One of the nurses said she was sure Todd already had all the angels in heaven laughing. One of the doctors responded that he probably already had a basketball game started.

THE VISITATION

For the next two days and nights, there was a steady and some-times very long line for visitation at the funeral home, at times reaching into the street. I was touched, moved, and sometimes surprised at how many persons from all lifestyles, from all ages and circumstances that had been inspired by Todd's life.

There were young children whom he had coached in Little League, church, and many others whom he had touched through his many youth activities, tears rolling from their eyes. There was a ninety-one year old woman, barely able to walk even with the assistance of her two children and a walker. She had insisted she leave the nursing facility to pay her respects to Todd.

Once I looked down the line that was still forming out onto the street. I saw a man who had founded a company that later became a Fortune 500 company. Behind him were a mother and son, typically known as *street people*. She had on several layers of clothing. He carried a paper sack with some of their few posses-sions. At first, I did not understand the tears in her eyes. Then she told me that one day Todd had stopped to give them a ride as they walked along side the highway. He said he was going to lunch and asked if they had time to go with him. She continued, "He bought us the biggest meal I've ever eaten. He treated us like we were his friends."

Another woman shared how Todd touched her friend. Todd had placed an ad to sell a washing machine. Her friend went to see it. Todd knew the friend and her difficult living situation. He sold her the washer. Later, when her friend proudly showed her purchase, she said she paid only fifteen dollars for it. The woman said she knew, at that moment, Todd actually gave her the washer. He only charged her the fifteen dollars to save her friend's pride. This woman did not know Todd personally. She said she came to pay her respects, because "a man like Todd deserved respect."

During visitation, I heard incidents about Todd that I never knew. Some brought tears, more brought laughter. I feel that, perhaps, God gave Todd those bonus years in order to touch more lives. Later, when I learned that matching lungs were found five days after his death, I felt that Todd had fulfilled God's plan for his life and had taken him from his suffering to his reward. I still do not understand why, but I remember Todd saying that we do not need to know all the whys. We just need to rely on our faith.

THE FINAL GOODBYE

Todd's funeral was held in the largest church in our county. It seated five hundred. Still, it was not large enough to accommodate the overflow crowd. They had to bring in extra seating. It was the church where Todd taught Sunday school. It was where Todd sang in the choir. It was where Todd chaperoned youth trips and where he served as a deacon. It was, also, where he was married at that same altar, on that exact date, ten months earlier.

The same men who served Todd as groomsmen on the happiest day of his life now served him as pallbearers on my saddest day.

I had sometimes wondered if I would find the strength to walk behind Todd's casket. My mind told me I might have to do that. My heart said I never would. I think God used a song to help me with that difficult task.

Just before Todd's death, Vince Gill released the song, "Go Rest High on That Mountain," which he had written in memory of his brother. I had not heard about the song, but Angela heard it on the radio as she drove to Lexington earlier that week. She requested the song be played as we entered the church. As I walked down the church aisle, hearing that beautiful song for the first time, I felt as if the angels were walking beside me. Once again, God showed me his love and strength when I needed it the most.

THE FIRST CHRISTMAS WITHOUT TODD

In most areas, Todd was mature far beyond his age, but not at Christmas! From early childhood, [okay, I will admit waking him really early Christmas morning, even before he knew about Santa] Todd would want to get up at three or four in the morning. One time he got up at two to see what Santa brought. I would not allow him to come down the stairs until both girls were up. Hope was easy to wake. All he had to say was, "Santa came," and she was up. Angela, however, was another story. She thought if there were gifts from Santa at three, they would still be there when she got up at a decent hour.

One year, Todd asked Santa for an Atari. While I put together a toy kitchen set for Hope and arranged their Santa gifts, Donald was *testing* the Atari game. We did not realize that Todd was awake listening to that ping-pong sound of the game. When we were ready for bed, about two o'clock a.m., Todd came running down the stairs followed by two sleepy sisters, shouting, "Santa came! Santa came!"

Even as an adult, he retained that kid-like excitement about Christmas. When he was twenty-six, he asked me to buy him a train set for Christmas. I told him that I refused to buy a grown man a toy. On Christmas morning, Todd was under the tree shaking all the presents trying to find his train. He would shake a box and ask, "Is this my train, Mama?" He would pick up what he knew was a shirt size box, shake it, and ask the same question to every present under the tree. He was shaking every gift regardless of its size or shape, asking, "Is this my train, Mama?" I had hidden the train in another room and just placed a few, smaller gifts for him under the tree. "Boy, this must have been a hard year for Santa. I just have two little boxes," Todd stated.

After we opened all the presents, Todd asked, "Where's my train, Mama?" I reminded him that I refused to buy him one. He burst into laughter. He explained that earlier in the week he had come by my house, and finding the door unlocked, he walked in. On the couch, unwrapped, lay his train. Even as a child, he was difficult to surprise. However, part of his joy was pretending that he was.

Then came the Christmas I had dreaded for twenty-five years, my first Christmas without Todd. I remembered that first Christmas after the diagnosis. Both children were hospitalized with pneumonia, and I was going through the motions of Christmas with a heavy heart. I wondered if either child would live to see another Christmas. We were baking cookies for Santa and remembering a television commercial, Todd said, "Guess what, Mama, we're baking memories." A small child's words reminded me that one day all I would have was memories, and I could not waste one minute making them. His words gave me back my Christmas joy, and we had a wonderful Christmas.

Each year, in the recesses of my mind, I questioned if I might lose Todd before the next Christmas. I knew the season would never again be as joyous, the lights on the tree never again as luminous if Todd was not here to share them with me. I often questioned if I could even celebrate the season without him.

Twenty-five Christmases had come and gone and oh, the memories we made. But they were not enough to sooth the pain I was feeling as I faced my first Christmas without my son.

Christmas Eve '95 was on a Sunday. I attended church, but not necessarily to celebrate the birth of Jesus, but to have something to fill my time. I planned to pick up Angela and her husband, Craig, at the airport at eight o'clock p.m. when they returned from their honeymoon. They had married the Saturday before in the same church where Todd and his bride had married the previous year on the same day. Angela had contemplated canceling her big church wedding. Todd was supposed to escort her down the aisle, and she felt it would be impossible to proceed with her plans. I knew Todd would have said, "Angela, I had my big day, now it's your turn."

I had put aside my grief so I could participate in pre-wedding activities, but now there was nothing to distract me from feeling my pain. My youngest child, Hope, and her finance were spending the day with her father and his mother. I felt so alone. To be honest, I was indulging in a major pity party.

Since my divorce in '83, after twenty years of marriage, I was accustomed to being alone part of the day. However, even after the children became adults, they returned to my home on Christmas Eve night to wait for Santa Christmas morning. Now I had to face the day I had so long dreaded. But how? Twenty-five years of living with CF still had not prepared me to face that moment. I realized that nothing could prepare a parent for the death of a child.

I do not remember anything about the church service. I do not even remember praying, but isn't that one of the great things about God? He often answers without our asking. Later that day, he revealed his presence to me through a life-changing experience.

It was a sixty-mile drive to the airport, so I decided to go to the Opryland Hotel to fill my time. The hotel is a Nashville, TN attraction, known for the thousands of Christmas lights and decorations throughout its magnificent gardens. Todd had taken me there two years before, and we shared a special time together. I soon questioned the sanity of my decision and realized that beautiful decorations and exotic flowers could not fill my void. I remembered that first Christmas after the CF diagnosis when Todd referred to the "baking memories," but now memories just hurt. Still, it was all I had left of Todd, so I opened the gift of memory.

I was not questioning God about Todd's death. No, I did not ask God, "Why?" I often had in the beginning, but God answered that question through Todd by the way he lived. I realized that God had given us many bonus years and memories, but as I sat in a secluded spot that I found in one of the hotel's gardens, my pent-up grief burst forth like a broken dam.

Christmas Eve, alone, sitting in the middle of a manufactured paradise, I was feeling despair. I looked toward heaven and said, "Oh, Todd, I wish you could see how beautiful this is!"

Suddenly, yes, instantly, I felt an indescribable peace and the thought, "Oh Mom, that's nothing compared to what I'm seeing up here!" Then I realized that I was just celebrating Jesus's birthday down here. Todd was there actually celebrating with Jesus in heaven. My tears immediately stopped, and I spent the remainder of the day enjoying myself with a new, unique Christmas spirit.

What had happened? I cannot explain that. Was Todd's spirit speaking to me? Was God sending me a special message? I do not know what it was, but I do know what it was not. It was not anything that I thought or did.

My son was still dead to earth, but I knew he was alive in heaven. I was still at the hotel alone, yet I have never felt God's presence more real. I realized Christmas is not a date on the calendar, but a season in the heart, a season to celebrate each day, because Jesus was born and still lives.

When the Christmas season approaches and I begin to miss Todd, all I have to do is remember the peace God gave me so long ago. It changed forever the way I approach Christmas. It changed forever the way I view life.

Note: I am including the following newspaper column, because I believe it will give you, the reader, a truer picture of Todd the adult, with the little-boy joy of Christmas.

DECEMBER 20, 1990

SCOOP SOUNDS OFF

Christmas is my favorite time of the year. It's the only night of the year that you can count on something special happening. It's the one night that reindeer can fly and a jolly elf, named Santa, can make wishes come true. It's when a snowman named "Frosty" never melts and when "Grinches" always return Christmas. But more importantly, it's when we're a little nicer, more understanding, and more caring about each other. It's not just another night of the year. There's something different about Christmas Eve. Christmas has always been associated with miracles because that's what Christmas is. It's the story of a virgin who gave birth to a king in a stable. It's when the shepherds followed a star that no one else could see to Bethlehem to find the Savior. It's when wise men, both then and now, worship the birth of a baby. All miracles.

We have mixed the two stories of Jesus and Santa so much that it's often hard to interpret one from the other. Christmas has become so commercial that we forget why we celebrate the occasion. We are so busy in seeing the presents that we forget to see the gift. We are so busy running from one gathering to the next that we forget to stop and see the real meaning of Christmas.

I like getting presents as much as anyone. On Christmas Eve it always was, and still is, off to Granny and Granddad's house. Granny cooks enough to feed our family, the shepherds, wise men, and anyone else who happened to be at the stable on that special night. Then after dinner, it's a semi-organized opening of the presents. The grandkids, all five of us, already know which gifts are ours. I'm the oldest, at twenty-six, while the youngest one is sixteen. But when we're at our grandparents house, we're kids again. Granny and Granddad sit in the corner. Granny smiles as we open the gifts she bought us. Granddad is always surprised at the gifts he selected for us. And he always acts surprised and happy with the presents we bought him, although he doesn't always know what they are or how he's going to use them. But that doesn't matter, they're from his grandkids, and that's all that matters.

But that's not the end of the night; it's only beginning, because Christmas Eve isn't just any night. It's *that* night when *he* comes.

I can still remember waiting in line to see "the big guy in the red suit" and instructing Angela and Hope on the do's and don'ts of Santa etiquette. I remember telling him what I wanted for Christmas and then waiting for that special morning when wishes came true. I can still remember how hard it was to fall asleep and how it was even harder to wake up my sisters to tell them that *he* had come during the night. I still remember how Mom and Dad would sit back on Christmas morning, with their sleepy smiles, and watch us open our gifts. Hope and I would play with our new toys. Angela would go back to bed. Dad would watch television and Mom would *attempt* to cook breakfast. [One of her better meals]

Then later in the morning, Mom always insisted that we stop what we were doing while she read the Christmas Story from Luke. She did this every year, and the story was always the same. But we would humor her and listen because Santa might still be watching. Now I realize how important those readings were. That was the true meaning of Christmas that we somehow lost in all the confusion. And we still do.

UNEXPLAINED
EXPERIENCES

In addition to the experience at Opryland Hotel, the first Christmas after Todd died, I have had two other experiences where I felt Todd's presence so close it was as if he was still alive. I do not understand them and cannot explain how they happened. I hear others speak of dreaming about their loved ones who have passed. I never dream about Todd, although I wish I did. I know that some people believe our loved ones can communicate with us from the other side. I am a skeptic, but I also often question God's whispers. He usually has to *hit me over the head* to get my attention. Regardless of the how or why, whether it was just my imagination or Todd was really communicating with me, I have felt Todd's presence strongly on two other occasions.

Shortly after Todd married, he asked me to come to his house to see "The Lion King." He had watched it and said it was one of the best movies ever. I declined the invitation telling him I did not enjoy animated movies and besides, he and Sarah were newlyweds and needed time alone. He continued begging and when he promised he would cook my dinner, I accepted. Todd was a good cook. It was an enjoyable evening and became one of the last special moments we shared outside the hospital. I agreed the movie was one of the best I had seen.

A few years after his death, Hope took me to New York to see the Broadway version. My children had always heard me say that one of my dreams was to see a Broadway play. She had obtained aisle seats on the second row. The theater, set, actors, and music made it everything of which I had dreamed. Throughout the play, I kept remembering the day I spent watching the movie version with Todd. I knew he would have been so happy for me that Hope had given me that experience and wished he were there to share it with me. At the end of the play, the cast members came down the aisle to join the others on stage. They were singing "The Circle of Life." It was then that I felt Todd's presence. I could almost hear him saying, "Mom, I am still a part of that circle. I am still with you."

I joined the rest of the audience in a standing ovation, but I was probably the only one with tears running down my face. They were tears of joy. Hope had made one of my dreams come true, and I felt somehow, some way, Todd was sharing that moment with me.

I had the third experience recently. Angela took me to meet my favorite celebrity, Trace Adkins. As the senior director of marketing and advertising for Dollar General, she had been working with him on their advertising campaign and arranged for me to spend some time with him before his segment at the Grand Ole Opry.

It was a bonus for me to learn that the Oak Ridge Boys were also appearing that night. They were Todd's favorite. The first song he played as a disc jockey was one of theirs. The last song he played on the radio, seven years later, was their song "Elvira." He really wanted to see them perform in person and on two occasions had tickets to their concert only to end up in the hospital both times.

As they were singing, I thought to myself, "Todd, I'm watching them for you." When they began their last song of the night, "Elvira," I had the oddest feeling as if Todd was seated right beside me. Was that last song a sign to me that Todd is always near me, still protecting me in death as he tried to do in life? I truly do not know, but those three experiences tend to make me believe that is so. Perhaps I should do as Todd did, and not question the *why*.

TODD'S RAINBOW

Todd had a special love for rainbows. As a child, I can remember my mother stopping her work to take me outside whenever a rainbow appeared and relating the story of the promise God sent after he destroyed the world with a flood. I did the same with my children. However, Todd was the child who developed a special appreciation for this display of nature.

Often, when he was just a little boy and he saw a rainbow, he would rush into the house and insist I stop whatever I was doing to go see the rainbow with him. I remember one very special rainbow moment with Todd. He and Angela were attending the high school where I taught. That morning we were running late, and I was in a hurry. With the school in sight, Todd spotted a rainbow and said, "Mom, look, there's a rainbow."

I was driving and answered I could not drive and look. He said, "Then pull off the road." Afraid I would be late for school, I told him I didn't have the time. He answered, "Mom, you can always make time to stop and look at a rainbow." We pulled off, got out of the car, and shared a moment I will always cherish. From that moment on, I have always taken time to stop, look, and enjoy the beauty of a rainbow.

After a hard rain threatened Angela's Kentucky Derby party she planned for weeks, a neighbor called her house to tell her to go outside and look at the beautiful rainbow that had just appeared. As she stood telling her two-year-old son the story about God's promise, tears filled my eyes as I remembered all the times I had done the same thing with Todd, but they were not tears of sadness, just wonderful memories.

I realized the rainbow is more than a symbol that God will never destroy the earth with water again. I have come to view it as God's promise that regardless of the storms of life, if we will trust in him, he will turn our adversities into something beautiful.

That he did for me. Two years after Todd's death, God sent my first rainbow, my first grandchild, Hurley Calister Turner IV; twenty-two months later I was blessed with a second rainbow, Todd Alexander Turner; then four years later a third, William Craig Turner; fifteen months later my fourth rainbow, Jacob Connor Martin. They have brought me happiness and joy I once thought I would never feel again after Todd died, proving that God always gives us back more than he takes.

Todd's life was not one of a child born with a fatal illness and endured. His was a journey lived with laughter, determination, responsibility, love, friendship, faith, and a life lived to the very fullest. He just happened to have cystic fibrosis. He was never its victim in life. He accomplished that by giving to the world and making a positive impact with the thirty-one years he had.

Naturally, I miss Todd and think about him each day, but not with grief. Whenever I remember him, it is rarely through tears or sadness, but with smiles and laughter. Todd showed me how to do that. He taught me how to live, believe, and overcome obstacles while laughing through it all. He also taught me how to face death. I can honestly say I see the rainbows of Todd's life more than the storms.

Todd said earlier in his writing that he never questioned God why he had cystic fibrosis, but he often wondered why he was still alive after all his friends had died. I have learned from him not to question God why he gave me this remarkable son for such a short time; however, I do sometimes wonder why I was so blessed to be his mother and share his remarkable journey.

We thought a lung transplant would be the *miracle* in Todd's life. Later, I realized that the *true miracle* was with us all the time. It was Todd himself and the way he lived.

PART III
TODD'S JOURNEY
THROUGH THE EYES OF
HIS COMMUNITY

Note: This section contains tributes written by persons representing various areas of Todd's life. They capture his spirit as a student, friend, co-worker, community leader, patient, and Christian. I asked these persons to share, because I did not want the reader to picture Todd only through his viewpoint or a mother's perspective.

TODD'S JOURNEY

THROUGH THE EYES
OF HIS TEACHER

LANA JO STONE,
ENGLISH AND SPEECH TEACHER, ALLEN
COUNTY SCOTTSVILLE HIGH SCHOOL

Over the past thirty plus years, I have had both the honor and the pleasure to share the lives of some of the most remarkable young people that God has ever placed upon this planet. You see I have taught high school English to literally hundreds of these young minds.

Each of them has arrived in my classroom carrying their own unique talents and abilities, and each of them has come with their own personal tale to tell. All of them have taught me far more than I have ever taught them, and some of the more *special* have left imprints upon my very soul.

Early in my teaching career, I was especially blessed to have the opportunity to work with a young man named Todd Gibbs. Todd was a victim of cystic fibrosis, and while the disease had already taken its toll on his physical stature [he was very petite in size and often suffered long stays in which he was hospitalized due to problems with labored breathing and horrible seizures of uncontrollable coughing], the fiend, CF, could not touch his sweet spirit.

I remember the very first day that Todd came to my class as if it were yesterday. He might have been small, but his heart was enormous and his presence radiated throughout my room, engulfing both myself and the other students. He never felt sorry for himself, and after you came to know him, you could not feel sorry for him either.

Even on extremely bad days, Todd smiled. The child did not seem to know how to stop smiling. He bore no bitterness toward God, medicine, or any other human being. He was chosen to bear this cross and, by George, he was going to make the best of it.

Todd would accept nothing less than his best in every endeavor. He would not believe that he had limitations from doing anything that anyone else might do. He had no fear of attempting those obstacles from which other teenagers might shy away. He would chart his course, make his strategy, and meet every goal head on. If he ever experienced fear, no one could detect it. If he ever met failure, I do not think he knew it, because if something went against his original calculations, he would simply rethink his steps and proceed in another direction.

Todd commanded respect, because he was respect. He understood his role in this old world and not only did he accept it, I often thought that he felt sorry for those of us who failed to see the true beauty of life while we were actually living it. He knew that his days were literally numbered in this world, and he was not about to waste one precious second of the life he had been given. He might die at a young age, but he was not going to die until he had lived life to the max.

In school, Todd was a typical teenager. He loved school. He wasn't too crazy about the studies, but he loved the social side of education. He had tons of friends. He enjoyed sports and clubs, and nothing gave him more joy than sharing those events with the people he loved. To this day, I can hear his sweet laughter in the halls of our building.

There was so much good about Todd that I suppose it could be considered hard to try to sum up his most admirable traits, but because he and I had such a close relationship, I believe that I can do so. You see, the thing that made Todd Gibbs such an inspiration to many others and me, was his unquestioning faith. If God had chosen him to live as an example for others during his many, many trials and tribulations, he would do so, and he would sing the praises of his creator each and every day. The longer he suffered with the disease, the stronger his faith became. He once told me that he couldn't be angry for having CF, because there were so many people who had far worse burdens to bear. Besides, he had been born in the greatest nation, in the most beautiful state, into the most wonderful home, and blessed with the best friends that a small rural community could provide. God had been good to him and he dare not act as if he were ungrateful.

Now, I know that Todd must have grown weary of his illness and of the limitations that it placed on his everyday existence, but he refused to surrender to self-pity. He figured he had two choices. He could lie down and feel sorry for himself until his time was over, or he could get up and make a difference while he was alive. He decided to make a difference, and I have never known anyone who could have made more of a difference than this beautiful, courageous, young man did.

Everyone who ever met Todd Gibbs knows for sure that their life was a little richer by the hours, days, and years that they shared with him. Each of them was given the rare opportunity to see the wonder of life through the eyes of someone who cherished every single second they lived. They were taught that life doesn't have to be just what we think it should be to be revered and cherished. Even the times of trial and stress have their purpose and true beauty can be found within them. They learned that with family and friends there really aren't any obstacles that one cannot endure. They were given insight into the very essence of life.

In the years after Todd left my classroom, and before his untimely death, we remained close. He would often return to our school for one occasion or another, and he would always rush to remind me of how much I had helped him with his education.

At each of these times, I would chuckle to myself that he should feel that I had taught him anything, for he had been the teacher, not only for me, but also for so very many others.

Now that Todd has been deceased for fourteen years, and after I too have been called upon to bear one of life's very hardest trials, [the death of my eldest daughter], I believe that I have come to be somewhat more like that precious little boy who first taught me that, indeed, bad things do happen to good people. We do not have to understand every thing that happens to us in this life, because each of us has a purpose in God's great universe. The best thing for any of us to do is to do what Todd did. Todd didn't spend his time worrying about how long he had to live. He spent his time worrying about living the time he had.

TODD'S JOURNEY

THROUGH THE EYES
OF HIS COACH

BY DAVID YOUNG

The life of Todd Gibbs would not be complete without mention-
ing Lady Patriot basketball. Starting in the spring of 1977, TG
was synonymous with the Lady Patriots. I remember that spring
day, sitting in the old Allen County High gym, known as the
Middle School then. I was supervising break time for four hundred seventh and eighth graders. During that time, there were
usually at least five games of full-court basketball with all side
goals being used.

While watching with amusement, that no one was getting
hurt and every player knew who was on his or her team, I felt
a tap on my shoulder. I turned to see Todd standing eye level
with me. Of course, I was seated on the second row and Todd
was standing on the floor! He wanted to know if he could be a
Lady Patriot manager. Knowing that Todd was battling the cruel
disease of cystic fibrosis, I did not want to discourage him or
damage his aspirations, but I did want him to know how difficult
the job would be and exactly what was expected of a member of
the Lady Patriot family. Without blinking an eye and with a stare
that would have convinced anyone never to doubt this young

man's determination to accomplish his goals, Todd answered firmly, "I can and *will* do whatever it takes."

From the start, Todd was a perfect fit for the Lady Patriot program and for me. It did not take long for Todd to enter my heart and never leave. He became like a son to me. From that day, until his final breath, we would be the closest of friends with so many memories to cherish.

Early on, we became comfortable with each other, joking, laughing, and being serious when needed, especially during practices.

Todd took a lot of pressure off me by doing all the pre-practice, time-consuming duties I had been doing, like rolling goals up and down, getting water bottles filled, mopping floors, and making sure the basketballs were at the right gym. Before he graduated, Todd even went to WKU's athletic training camp and added taping ankles to his list of services, providing me even more time to prepare practice and game plans.

Off the court, our friendship grew as well, and one important event really cemented our bond. During one of his extended hospital stays, Todd kept a registry of all who visited him. When he went home, he tore the names apart and had a drawing for a Dalmatian pup. Of course, my name was drawn, and I could not say no. Karen and I named the dog T.G. [Some of you may remember the three-legged dog that frequently made his way to the high school in the late seventies.]

In spite of all the duties he already had, Todd kept l o o k i n g for something else to do to help me. After the second year, Todd began to delegate some of the prep work to other managers so he could be more available to assist me with pre and post-game responsibilities. He made sure all players, managers, and cheerleaders were on the bus, called Mickie D's to let them know we were on our way, and made sure all equipment and supplies made it back to school. Todd would always wait with me until each girl was picked up by her parents. Then, we would take our number one fan, a man who was mute, Winfred Jones, home when no one was going his way.

Those were good years; winning seasons, invitational tourneys with overnight stays [especially the LIT (Louisville Invitational Tournament) championship], district and region championships, and a State Tournament trip. Todd was as integral a part of that success as any coach or player.

Todd and I remained close and shared many special days and occasions after the basketball years. Karen and I had our first child on January 10, 1981 and, of course, Todd became her adopted big brother. He would always check to make sure Karen and Sarah had what they needed before leaving for games. Four years later, Susan was born and, once again, even though Todd had graduated in May of 1984, he welcomed the addition to *our* family.

At Christmas, he never missed stopping by to see the girls. To this day, a Christmas Eve does not go by that Todd's name is not mentioned. He loved seeing the excitement of our girls on this special night. The sparkle in his eyes and the drama in his voice as he would explain to the girls how the radar at the radio station had shown the location of Santa Claus, hypnotized all of us. Throughout the years, Todd was the watchful eyes of a big brother on many church trips our children took. When he married, I was honored to be a groomsman for my true and trusted friend.

By the '83 basketball season, Todd kept his close ties to the Lady Patriot program by taking over for long time "Voice of the Patriots," Danny Tabor, and began a three-year stint as the play-by-play announcer of the Patriots. Todd also became manager of the Lady of the South Tournament that Danny and I had begun, because Danny wanted us to be able to stay close to home during the holiday season. It did not take Todd long to expand the LIS [Lady Invitational of the South] to a sixteen-team tournament known all over the south central United States as one of the best. Then, of all things, Todd decided to continue his ties with all the girls' programs in the region by getting his officiating license. He was quick to learn that officiating could cause stress in friendships, but if you knew Todd as we did, he had everyone believing that every call he made was the right one!

I could go on for a much longer time with Todd Gibbs' stories, but I need to close from the heart.

Purposely, I have only mentioned cystic fibrosis a couple of times during this tribute. Everyone knew Todd had this devastating disease. However, he did not want anyone giving in to him because of it. He did not want to be defined by CF. I want everyone to know about Todd's determination in battling CF. He was in and out of hospitals, on breathing machines, and participating in all the trial medicines he had to take while keeping a great outlook on life. He always maintained his faith in God, and persevered to live and battle the disease as long as he could.

For all Todd Gibbs did for me as a basketball coach and friend, he taught me more than he learned from me. Through him, I saw how thoughtfulness, kindness, trust, faith, and friendship should be an everyday part of life. Most of all, I learned how life is not about what you *cannot do* but what you *determine to do.*

Little did I know then how my life would be enriched by that tap on the shoulder.

TODD'S JOURNEY

THROUGH THE EYES
OF HIS RESPIRATORY
THERAPIST AND FRIEND

BY LADAWN REYNOLDS BA RRT
SENIOR RESPIRATORY THERAPIST
HYPERBARIC MEDICINE UNIVERSITY
OF KENTUCKY HOSPITAL

When LaRecea contacted me about doing a tribute for Todd, I thought, "What can I say that will do him justice?" My primary concern was I wanted to make sure everyone knew what a wonderful person Todd really was. For those that knew him it was a no-brainier, but for those who did not, I wanted them to see him as I did.

We first met when Todd was my patient at the University of Kentucky Hospital. I do not even remember when our therapist/patient relationship turned into a special friendship. Todd was just so personable that you could not help but like him. He was a unique person who drew everyone in and then he had you for life. I would spend hours in his room doing his treatment, watching UK basketball, and talking about anything and everything. It did not matter if I was working or not, if Todd was in the hospital, I was there as much as possible.

Todd loved his Allen County girls' basketball team, their coach and his role as organizer of the annual girls' basketball invitational tournament in Scottsville. Until that time, girls' basketball was never much of a priority for me. I had always considered basketball a boys' sport. Todd changed my way of thinking. I was able to meet the coach and listen to their stories. The minute the annual tournament was finished, Todd was already working on the list of teams for the following year. He was excited at the quality of teams he was able to get, particularly if they were from out of state, and especially if they were contacting him to get an invite. His work with girls' basketball did not end there. He also was a referee. I remember going to a game that he refereed and at the end, we had to be escorted from the gym because of angry fans. The losing team lost by at least thirty points! Girls' basketball—Todd loved it!

It seemed like anything that involved excitement and action, Todd was there. His work with the radio station gave him a lot of opportunity for that. He was called "Scoop," and he took it seriously. He was going to scoop out any and every news item he could find no matter the time, day or night. One time when I was visiting Todd, a call came out for a house fire. Off we went, in the middle of the night, in the winter! I was freezing and he was in his moment.

This sense of adventure even followed him to the hospital. Periodically he would get a pass, and I would take him out to eat or shop. One time we were at my place when a huge storm came through knocking out the power. Immediately after it ended, Todd wanted to drive around looking at the flooding, downed trees, and power lines. All I could think about was how Dr. Kanga was going to kill us both if he found out what we were doing.

He devoted himself to cystic fibrosis, the disease that brought us together at an early age. I remember going through one of his photo albums and seeing pictures of him as a youngster at the White House with his family. That focus shifted to organ donation as his disease became more progressed. I remember when he got on the lung donor list. He was happy and sad at the same time. He was happy for a chance at a new life with his new lungs, but sad that someone would have to lose their life in order to give him his. That was Todd, always thinking of others before himself. His devotion to the Kentucky Organ Donation Association inspired me to become an organ donor. Todd's work was never done.

Todd's biggest passion was outer space. His house was full of NASA memorabilia-like posters, books, pictures, and models. He even had the transcripts from the Challenger explosion inquiry. His biggest goal was to go up in one of the space shuttles. Our best adventure together was our trip to Florida to visit a friend and also to go to NASA. He loved it, just like a kid in a candy or toy store wanting to go here, there and everywhere. Every time I think about it, I remember how funny he was throughout the whole trip. I let him drive into NASA, and he got us into an area with all of these Restricted Area signs. I just knew we were going to be arrested, but he wanted to see how far we could get! On our deep sea-fishing excursion, Todd sat by the edge of the boat, and when we hit a wave, he would try to catch some of the spray in his mouth. His reasoning was that having CF, he was salt deficient and this would give him extra.

One thing Todd learned on that trip is that we females, especially me, need our sleep. The video that he made of the trip was labeled "Grumpy and Todd go to Florida." The whole trip is full of memories. I still have the NASA bell he gave me on display in my house. In keeping with his love of the moon and stars, for his last birthday I had a star named for him. Unfortunately, Todd died before I could ever give him his gift, but I know he is up there with them now.

Todd was always on the go and was never one to let the grass grow under his feet. I have so many other memories and stories I could share that this could go on forever. Let's just say that Todd was compassionate, loving, giving, warm, unique, wonderful, funny, personable, and any other adjective you can think of. Most of all, he was a very special friend. I miss him terribly and think of him often, but always with a smile on my face.

TODD'S JOURNEY

THROUGH THE EYES OF
HIS YOUTH PASTOR

BY KEN GOFORTH, MINISTER OF MUSIC,
SCOTTSVILLE BAPTIST CHURCH

A LITTLE MAN WITH A BIG HEART
My Memories of Todd Gibbs

When I began my ministry at Scottsville Baptist Church in August 1975, I certainly had no idea I would still be here thirty-four years later, and I certainly had no idea I would build such strong relationships with the people of this community. One of those wonderful relationships was forged with a young man named Todd Gibbs. From the first moment we met, I knew we were going to have a good time together.

Todd was one of those persons who came to church not from coercion, but because he truly loved being here. His infectious smile and his charming personality were always a welcome sight whether he was here for worship or just dropped by for a visit. Of course, underneath that was just enough mischief to keep me guessing.

Like most people who knew him, I was always amazed at the way he refused to let the disease that ravaged his lungs destroy his zest for life. I have never known another person who packed more living [in the best sense of the word] into thirty years of life. He inspired me to be better at my job, because I wanted him to have a good time when we were together. He made me understand the importance of living today, because we are not promised tomorrow.

Scottsville Baptist Church was one of the most important segments of Todd's life. He spent many hours involved in ministry here and in our many mission trips.

He was involved in our children's ministries, our youth ministries, and, after graduation from high school, he became a leader in both of those ministries. As a Sunday school teacher and Vacation Bible School leader, he positively influenced the lives of many of our children and youth. His name often comes up in our conversations about the church folks we most remember.

Some of my fondest memories of Todd are found in those times we spent away from church at camps, concerts, and mission opportunities. Because of my advancing years, some of the chronology of the events has escaped me, but the joy these memories bring is as real as ever.

CAMP JOY

Since 1975, I have been the director of Music Week at Camp Joy, a Baptist assembly located in Brownsville, Kentucky. For one week each summer, I have loaded up the church van [or bus] and taken our fourth through eighth graders for a week of music, Bible study, and fun. As a young teenager, Todd spent several of these weeks with me. There are so many memories of these younger years that are wonderful, but the following two are priceless.

On one occasion, we had a male camper with us who could not stay out of the girls' room. He would get up each morning before everyone else and sneak down to the other dorm. The girls complained to Todd about this situation, so he gathered up some washcloths and some wire and waited for his opportunity. When we went to bed that evening, Todd and some of his buddies pretended to be asleep until they were certain the culprit was sleeping soundly. They then slipped out their bunks and proceeded to wrap the washcloths around his wrists and ankles, wrap the wire around the cloths, and wire his appendages to the bed. When he awakened, he was unable to move. While he was restrained, the other boys explained to him the error of his ways, and threatened him with even worse punishment if he continued. They kept him in that position until well into the morning, and only released him after profuse begging and a promise to never return to the girl's dorm.

The other memory involves a musical entitled "The Rainbow Express," which told the story of Noah and the ark. For this presentation, we built an elaborate set that included a large boat with a door in the side for loading the animals. Todd and a young lady from Russellville were the main characters for the play. They were dressed as his and her ladybugs. They narrated the story of how Noah built the ark and then filled it with a male and female of each species. We had stuffed animals for props, and they would take them into the ark. Two of the stuffed animals were rabbits, and, without my knowledge, Todd had several people bring small stuffed rabbits on the day of the performance. He had hidden those little rabbits throughout the ark and, when it came time to bring the animals off the ark, he walked out carrying not two, but ten or twelve little bunnies. Needless to say, the entire audience broke out in spontaneous laughter. Todd and I were so tickled at one another, it took several minutes for us regain our composure so we could go on with the musical. The sight of that boy dressed as a ladybug holding all those stuffed rabbits will forever be etched in my mind.

YOUTH TRIPS

My two Todds, Gibbs and Hurt, were the mainstays of the youth ministry during their high school days. I was trying to figure out how to do youth ministry and, whatever I tried, they were there with me. One of the very first extended trips we shared was a youth retreat in Panama City Beach, Florida. It was a great time of fellowship and Christian growth during those days together on the beach. One particular activity I remember involved a greased watermelon and the swimming pool. Two teams worked for a long time trying to get the watermelon across the pool and onto the deck. Todd Gibbs turned out to be one who finally pushed that greased watermelon onto the deck, and, after scoring the winning goal, he promptly *spiked* the watermelon. It, of course, burst into pieces and everyone there burst into laughter.

Todd had such a good time, he momentarily forgot about his limited breathing capacity. A few minutes later, however, he was lying beside the pool obviously having difficulty breathing. I leaned over and asked him how was doing. Todd replied, "Goforth, all this fun could just kill you!" I cannot begin to tell you how often this phrase has been repeated throughout the years.

ACSHS BAND

In addition to our relationship at church, Todd and I shared many enjoyable [and not so enjoyable] times with the Allen County-Scottsville High School Band. While Todd was in high school, I went with the band to Camp Crescendo for marching band training. One great moment from that experience involved a young cymbal player who had an aversion to cleanliness. Everyone told him to take a shower, but he found creative ways to avoid the cleansing water.

Todd came up with the ultimate scheme to get this young man in the shower. While we were practicing one afternoon, Todd walked over to him and said, "Your cymbals are out of tune. You have got to tune those things." When the unclean one asked how to do that, Todd responded, "You have to get in the shower with the cymbals and rub them while running hot water over them. I'll stand outside the shower and have you tap on the cymbal and I can tell when it is in tune."

That evening when we finished practice, Todd helped him to remove the grips from the cymbals and watched as he climbed into the shower with cymbals in hand. For approximately thirty minutes Todd would say, "Rub them a little more, you've just about got it." Not only did we get a clean drummer, but we also got *tuned* cymbals for the band.

In the summer of 1990, Todd and I, along with other adults, served as chaperones for the band as they traveled to Philadelphia to march in the July 4th Freedom Festival Parade. On the bus ride to Pennsylvania, Todd and one of his college friends were discussing the concept of freedom. The other young man shared that he thought it perfectly acceptable for a person to burn an American flag. Todd was in complete disagreement, and expressed his disdain for that idea. There was no animosity, but it was obvious the two were diametrically opposed. On the day of the parade as the band was getting into formation in the staging area, a very large and imposing gentleman came to help us find our place in the parade lineup. He was wearing a t-shirt on which an American flag was imprinted and underneath were the words, "Go ahead, and try to burn this one." Todd immediately ran to his friend and shouted, "Now's your chance, just take that flag and burn it." It was quite a long time before we saw the friend again, and, when we did, we never heard another word about flag burning.

MISSION TRIPS

During the summers of 1992, 1993, and 1994 Todd served as chaperone for our youth mission trips to Myrtle Beach, Biloxi, and Washington, D.C. In each of these locations, our youth and chaperones led Backyard Bible Clubs for children and performed musical concerts in campgrounds, government housing projects, military institutions, and any other place that would let us share our program. Gibbs was always available to do whatever it took to make these mission efforts successful. One of the most important attributes in providing this kind of ministry is flexibility, and he never complained about what I asked him to do. I remember that he and Sam Kent must have made fifty trips to Wal-Mart in Biloxi to get snacks for the children in our Backyard Bible Clubs. We were leading four of these each day and it seemed we never had enough snacks, because each day we had more and more children involved. As we were leaving on the last day of our trip, Todd and I had to get off the bus and literally removed the children who were hanging on the side wanting to go home with us.

One of the most enjoyable trips for Todd was our mission trip to Ft. Myer, Virginia, next door to Arlington National Cemetery. Todd was working for the public radio station in Bowling Green at the time and was able to do a feature interview with the Protestant chaplain at Arlington about his ministry to families who go there to bury their loved ones. It was an excellent piece of work and I know that he loved putting it together. [The week before his death, Todd learned that he had have received an award from the state broadcasters for that particular work]. During that week, we performed at Ft. Myer, Ft. McNair, and the Pentagon. It was a thrilling experience for all of us. It was the last trip that Todd was able to take with us, and I really believe it could not have been more appropriate.

CHURCH MINISTRY

Todd became a leader in our children's Sunday school and Vacation Bible School. He, of course, was one of the most loved leaders that children ever had. A lot of that has to do with the fact that he never really grew up and, like Peter Pan, could always relate to children. He loved them just as they were, and he saw the potential in them. He made learning about the Bible fun and exciting. I often hear stories from his students [now young adults] who share the joy of being in one of his classes.

PERSONAL NOTES

I cannot begin to convey in these short pages the impact that Todd Gibbs had upon my life and my ministry. As a student, a friend, and a colleague his positive influence continues to touch me today. I often look through the pictures of all those activities and that wonderful smile and bright eyes remind me to stay faithful and not let the trivialities get me down. If Gibbs could keep that attitude with all the difficulty in his life, how can I complain? I truly feel his spirit will be a part of who I am, until I am privileged to see him again in heaven. Then we will reminisce and laugh just as we once did, and I will bring him up to date on all that he missed. I look forward to that time.

TODD'S JOURNEY

THROUGH THE EYES HIS FRIEND

BY REV. DONNIE MEADOR, PASTOR, FAITH BAPTIST CHURCH, SCOTTSVILLE, KY

It was Monday, January 6, 1986. I was twenty-two years old and, for the first time in my life, I was lying in a hospital. The doctors believed I was suffering from hepatitis. That was the preliminary diagnosis based on blood work and careful examination. I was told that a liver biopsy was needed to confirm hepatitis or, per- haps, something else. I will admit that cancer crossed my mind.

Being in a hospital, facing the unknown, was not something I was dealing with very well. I was scared, very scared. I was pray- ing. I was looking for answers. I was worried.

I agreed to the liver biopsy and it was scheduled for early Tuesday morning. However, what happened around six o'clock p.m. that Monday night left an impression in my mind that I will never ever forget. In a simple phone call, I realized the true meaning of friendship. Let me explain.

Six years earlier, God answered a prayer of mine and, in the process, brought into my life Todd Gibbs. I had heard of Todd for years, but prior to the fall of 1979, Todd was simply the kid with cystic fibrosis. I admit I had no clue what CF was. I actually believed at one time that CF was some sort of contagious disease instead of a disease based upon a genetic defect. I just knew that Todd had CF and recalled that he was not expected to live long.

I was a grade ahead of Todd in school. In my eighth grade year, our class discussed dedicating the Allen County Middle School's annual to Todd. We knew it had been a tough year for Todd, in and out of the hospital in his on-going battle with CF. However, we were told that we could not dedicate the annual to him. It had something to do with the fact that Todd was still alive, still battling, still fighting.

In the fall of 1979, I was in my junior year of high school. Todd was a girls' basketball trainer for the Allen County-Scottsville Lady Patriots. I loved Lady Patriot basketball simply because, at that time at ACS, the girls' basketball team was winning. During the first five years, the team posted a record of 100–15, appeared in three state tournaments, and was the talk of the town. I wanted to be a part of that team.

My dream came true when I had the opportunity to start keeping statistics for the Lady Patriots. God opening that door meant that I would be a manager alongside Todd. To be honest, Todd was not pleased that our coach, David Young, gave me the opportunity. However, over the course of a few weeks, Todd and I became friends.

We celebrated as the Lady Patriots climbed to the top of girl's basketball in Kentucky. We also cried when our hopes and dreams of a state championship came to an unexpected end with a heartbreaking regional loss. Basketball had brought Todd and me together.

Our friendship continued. The following year went quickly. Before I wanted it to be over, it was. Yet, my friendship with Todd was not. In fact, it was growing.

I will always remember the summer of 1981. July 11, was my birthday, and that Saturday evening began as a typical Saturday evening in July in Allen County. The county fair was underway; hence, I went to the fair. It was not long after I arrived at the fair that another friend tracked me down at the fairgrounds with terrible news. Todd was very sick. His CF had taken a turn for the worst, and Todd needed to go to Lexington for a hospital visit. According to Julie, Todd was refusing to go, and he needed his friends to go to his house in Holland and talk him into going.

I headed to Holland. When I arrived, Todd was on the couch, looking sick. His family was there, and before long, several other friends began to arrive. I remember being concerned while others did not seem too phased by what was happening. I finally learned that it was all a charade. You see, Todd was not a bit sick! It was all a well thought out act to get me to come to his home for a surprise birthday party. Only Todd would have gone to that length to give me an eighteenth birthday.

The following years were filled with great memories. The memories also included an occasional argument. In 1984, Todd and I were in Boone County in northern Kentucky. By then, Todd was working at the local radio station, WLCK, and doing play-by-play announcing of the Lady Patriot ball games. I was still keeping stats and in the winter of 1984, AC-S's basketball travels took us to Boone County for a tournament.

I had driven us to northern Kentucky. AC-S played and lost. I do not remember the exact details other than when we started home we began arguing. I cannot tell you why or over what, I just remember Todd was upset and so was I. We decided to go by Lexington to visit a friend. We made a quick stop, and then headed toward Scottsville.

We were barely speaking until Todd yells at me, "You are going the wrong way! You are going to get us killed!" I had somehow pulled onto a major parkway going into in-coming traffic. Luckily, I did not get us killed. When I finally got back in the right lanes, we were able to laugh and whatever we had argued about seemed a mute point.

Within a few days of that adventure, Todd was battling for his life. By this time, Todd was going to a doctor in Bowling Green instead of Lexington. It was a Monday night in February of 1982, when word came that the doctor had told Todd and the family that his CF had progressed to a point where no hope was left. Todd was given about a week to live.

I could not believe it. I walked into Todd's room at The Medical Center in Bowling Green not knowing what to say. My friend was dying. I recall learning that Todd had made a decision.

Todd had asked to go back to Lexington to the University of Kentucky Medical Center. He was looking for a change and a change would be forthcoming. Todd was transferred, and in a few days, began to show signs of recovery. By the grace of God and the medical knowledge of a new CF doctor, Jamshed Kanga, Todd pulled through.

A few days later, I went back to Lexington to bring Todd home. He was on his way to recovery, having beaten the odds yet again. In the summer of 1985, I began to lose weight. By the end of the year, I was having trouble keeping food down and my skin had a yellow coloring to it. I knew something was wrong, so did my mother, and so did others. Yet, I would not go to a doctor. Todd's mother convinced me to go.

My doctor took one look at me, suspected hepatitis, and sent me into isolation at the Allen County Hospital. One of my first visitors that afternoon, complete with the mask and gloves, was Todd. When doctors transferred me to a larger hospital, Todd, his mother, and sister were there for me. Tests results indicated I needed a liver biopsy. Todd's job as news director at WLCK-WVLE radio and an on-going relocation of the station prevented him from coming. However, he did not need to come. A phone call turned out to be all that was needed.

It was about six o'clock p.m. Todd called. I told him my doctor was going to perform the liver biopsy early Tuesday. I said I was scared and afraid. I did not know what would happen.

Todd replied, "Donnie, do you want to go to Lexington? They have the best doctors. If you want to go to Lexington, I will have you there in three hours. I'll come and get you and I'll have you in Lexington as quick as I can."

I replied that I did not know anyone or any doctors in Lexington. "Don't worry about that," Todd said. "My mom can call my doctor, and I'm sure he'll have someone waiting for us when we get there."

I decided not to take Todd up on the offer. I told him that I would go if I was not satisfied with the results the following day. I stayed in Bowling Green and underwent the biopsy the next morning. It confirmed the hepatitis. Within a couple of days, I was with Todd going to a ball game.

As I look back on that time, what I recall is that Todd was willing, willing to drop everything for me. Todd wasn't afraid, wasn't concerned with not being able to do his job, and wasn't worried about himself. It was that phone call, and the tone in his voice that still means the world to me. Todd was always willing to listen, to listen to me complain, cry, ramble, and ponder. Whatever the situation, Todd was there. It was a true blessing to have the opportunity to call Todd my friend.

The thing that was so special about Todd was that it did not matter who you were, what you had, or what you did. Todd cared. He cared about me. I was just a poor kid when Todd and I first met. He cared. He cared when he gave me a birthday party when no one else would. He cared by allowing me to tag along when he permitted me to assist him on ball games. He cared when I was sick. Todd cared enough to convince the radio station owner to give me a job. He cared when he allowed me to help him in building a world-class basketball tournament. Todd cared about me when I did not even care about myself.

When Todd decided to walk away from his seven-and-a-half year job at the radio station, he stated, "I have gone as far as I can go here." It was time to move on. Todd cared enough to suggest that I be given the opportunity to replace him at the station. When I did not get the opportunity, Todd cared enough to suggest, "Why don't you go back to college?"

Todd cared two years later when he, basically, spelled out what I needed to do to prove I deserved the news director's job at the radio station. It wasn't that he was telling me what to do. It was because he believed in me, believed that I could do the job, believed in me when so many others doubted.

Todd was always someone who really, really cared. It is still difficult to believe Todd is gone. Occasionally, I dream about him. Often I wonder what Todd would think about my finally getting married and becoming a minister. Many times, I find myself wishing Todd was here, giving me one person to talk to.

Todd was the kind of person that only comes along once in a lifetime. Miss you Todd.

LaRecea Gibbs

TODD'S JOURNEY

THROUGH THE EYES
OF HIS DOCTOR

*BY JAMSHED KANGA MD, PROFESSOR
AND CHIEF, DIVISION OF PEDIATRIC
PULMONOLOGY, DIRECTOR
OF CYSTIC FIBROSIS CENTER
UNIVERSITY OF KENTUCKY*

Every CF patient is special. Some are more special than others are. Todd Gibbs falls into the latter category.

Todd and his family were a legend at the University of Kentucky long before I joined the faculty in July of 1983. His cystic fibrosis physician went away on sabbatical. When he returned home after being away for a year, Todd had begun treatment with a pulmonologist closer to his home.

Todd was lost to UK as a patient for a year.

My first encounter with this still well remembered patient was when I received a call from a pulmonologist in Bowling Green saying that a CF patient was dying and that the family would like to transfer him to UK. We made the arrangements. To my surprise, it was the famous Todd Gibbs about whom I had heard so much. He was very sick and I was very scared. To meet this special UK patient under such circumstances was daunting for a new physician. I threw the book at him with everything I knew to do, and with Divine intervention and assistance, Todd recovered and went back home to Scottsville, KY. An everlasting friendship was born.

After his miraculous recovery, Todd convinced two of his cousins with CF to come to Lexington for their CF care. I thus became part of the family, and to this day, always have the warmest feelings for my family in Scottsville.

Over the years, Todd and I grew very close. With a disease like CF, one is often in the hospital, so we were able to spend a lot of time together. After rounds, I would frequently visit his hospital room, and we would talk about all sorts of things. I would try to convince him how to be a good patient and take care of himself, and he would tell me how to be a good doctor and not to keep nagging him. We talked, we joked, but most of all we enjoyed each other's company.

Todd wrote for the local paper under the pseudonym of "Scoop." He once wrote an article about his experience in the hospital and described me as someone who creeps into your room in the wee hours of the morning to draw your blood. When I pretended to be offended by the description, he said that was the truth of what he thought the first time he met me. I guess I have forgiven him for that first impression.

Not only did I become part of his family, he became part of mine. When I made rounds on weekends, my young children would occasionally accompany me for their "Special Day" with Daddy. While I made rounds, they played in the playroom. Then we would have a treat—lunch in the hospital cafeteria. [Patients frequently became nauseas after looking at the food, but my kids thought it was so good.] If they knew that Todd was in the hospital at the time, they would ask if they could visit him, and he frequently ended up babysitting them while I made rounds.

He was fun and played games with them. He also told them some stories that were not true. He told them "how mean their daddy was as he would not let poor Todd go home, and how much he missed his mom," etc. etc. The kids would then plead his case for the rest of the weekend, and I would be thinking, "Wait till I get my hands on that boy's neck. I am going to strangle him."

Todd and my children developed a special friendship. If my son had a soccer game on a Saturday morning, Todd would be up and ready to go by eight o'clock a.m. Now on other days, I would have to go in and wake him up to do his treatments and get on with his day. After I finished rounds, we would drive out to watch the game. We both enjoyed being together outside the hospital, especially him after being cooped up in a hospital room for fourteen days.

One time at a game, my son kicked a beautiful shot towards the goal that missed by a fraction of an inch, and in my excitement, I shouted the "S" word. No matter how much I tried to convince Todd that I said "shucks," he could not be fooled. The next day, the whole CF team and every CF patient that was in the hospital at the time learned of my indiscretion.

Todd as a patient was also a teacher for numerous medical students and residents. Each time he would come across a young physician in training, he would try to help them become better. He felt that was his mission. "Your hands are too cold or you need to talk 'to,' and not 'at' your patients" were frequent bits of advice he would give them. He would help me evaluate students and residents by giving me feedback on how they performed when I was not there. This in turn helped me help them improve or give them positive feedback when they did something well. Young physicians loved Todd, as he had so much knowledge about the disease, hospitals, medicine, and life in general.

Todd was vertically challenged, but his handsome face and the twinkle in his eyes made up for his lack of height. Todd was irresistible to women, especially the young nursing staff. In all the years that I knew him, he was always dating a beautiful girl. He frequently brought them to his clinic visits, and they sure came to visit him when he was in the hospital. During one of our clinical co-relations classes, I had him speak on his perspectives of living with cystic fibrosis. It was a big event speaking in front of over a hundred medical students; however, as always,

Todd was calm and cool and had brought his beautiful, then current, girlfriend. The class went great and Todd, as always, did a wonderful job. I think every female medical student fell in love with him that day. His girlfriend was unusually quiet, but she sat through the entire hour-long class. A few weeks later, Todd informed me that they had broken up. I immediately asked him if it had to do with the lecture. He hesitated but then said, "She thought she knew about living with CF, but after the class the reality of the disease really hit home." In a way, he was glad that it happened and it happened again on several occasions. CF is a terribly difficult disease to live with, not only on the person with the disease, but on everyone around that person.

The next most memorable event in my life regarding Todd was the day of his graduation from college. I remember the big gymnasium where the event was held at Western Kentucky University in Bowling Green, KY. We almost didn't make it. Boy, did we get lost trying to find the place! My family was with me, and we cheered and cheered when Todd's name was called. From way up in the arena, I followed his every move and saw him toss his cap and tassel into the air.

At the end of the evening, he presented me with the cap on which he had written in white ink, "Kanga, without you this would not have been possible. Thanks. Todd Gibbs, WKU 1994, College Graduation." It was hard holding back the tears.

When Todd met the love of his life, he announced his wedding plans. Our family again traveled to Scottsville. The rehearsal dinner was so wonderful with the very close family. I was able to meet his lovely sisters, many cousins, uncles, aunts, and friends. There were laughter and tears as each one shared a story. Todd was in his element and so, so happy. He was glowing. The next day, I wore a tuxedo for the first time in my life since I was part of the wedding party. Todd was looking handsome with a beautiful smile across his face. The church wedding and the dinner afterwards were beautiful. Our family had the best time that weekend and my kids, now grown adults, still talk about it.

As Todd prepared to settle down to a happy, blissful married life, his disease started to worsen and he required more frequent hospitalizations. Then came a time when every breath was difficult. Todd knew he could not go on like that much longer. He started to look at the options and decided that he would like to go for a lung transplant. This renewed his hope and he worked hard to stay well, but his lungs just kept getting worse. Todd gradually could not breathe, and was placed on a ventilator to keep him going, hoping every day that a set of lungs would come. Unfortunately, this was not to be. Like many patients who are waiting for a transplant, Todd died in the ICU hooked up to a ventilator. After having been at his graduation and wedding just a short time before, I was heartbroken at being asked to be a pall-bearer at his funeral. It was a cold and very sorrowful day when I had to say goodbye to my very special friend from Scottsville, Kentucky.

It is hard to describe Todd. Words such as awesome, amazing, fascinating, adventurous, and determined come to mind. He went to school, he worked at the bank, he wrote for the newspaper, and he spoke on the radio. He volunteered for boy scouts, church, and various other organizations. He was a role model and a mentor to so many people young and old, well and sick, rich and poor. Todd never felt sorry for himself or asked, "Why did I have to have CF?" He always maintained that he was a better person because of his disease, and that he probably would not have been the person he was or had the opportunities he had, had he not had CF. Todd always looked at his glass as half-full, never half-empty. He made us all realize that having cystic fibrosis did not have to limit you in what you could do and achieve.

He was a popular master of ceremonies and a celebrity in his community. Along with his mother, LaRecea, he was a popular panelist at our CF Center's Annual Family Education Day. Together, they showed other families how CF could enrich one's life in ways that they had never imagined.

After his death, when I visited his home, the number of trophies and honors that Todd Gibbs had received awed me. There

Not a Wasted Breath

were pictures of him with the President and famous people from all over the country. This was a young man who had achieved more in his short life than most of us will in a dozen lifetimes.

Every CF patient is special to me, but Todd Gibbs will always be among the most special ones.

TODD'S JOURNEY

THROUGH THE EYES OF
HIS CO-WORKER

*SUBMITTED BY JEFF
YOUNGLOVE, DIRECTOR OF
CAMPUS AND COMMUNITY EVENTS,
WESTERN KENTUCKY UNIVERSITY*

"Live life every day to its fullest." Yes, it may seem like just another cliché, but that's how I remember Todd Gibbs, and that's how I've tried to emulate his zest for life since meeting him.

While maybe not daily, but at least more often than not, I strive to uphold that philosophy in my life since the time I began seeing Todd as someone very special.

My first introduction to Todd was through strictly verbal communication, and it wasn't until a few years later before I actually met him face-to-face. I was working as a graduate assistant for Radio-TV Services through Western Kentucky University's Office of Public Information, and Todd was working as news director for WVLE radio in Scottsville, Kentucky. I would provide audio news reports from Western and as a newcomer to the news area around Bowling Green, I always found Todd friendly and appreciative of what I was trying to accomplish in promoting Western activities. I didn't know it then, but it would be the beginning of a very special friendship and relationship established with him.

While working as Radio/TV Coordinator at Western, I considered some of the most important communities and areas that Western served and provided a backbone for its student population cities and counties such as Scottsville, Kentucky. After a few months of providing stories to various radio stations, I knew I could always count on getting our word out when I called Todd. He was a promoter of the university from the outset, and that would later prove a key ingredient to the professional opportunities at the university of which he contributed and became an important part.

After several years working at the local radio station, Todd indicated to me he had always wanted to pursue his college degree, and in 1989, he decided it was time to begin that journey. I had since become a fulltime employee at Western as Coordinator of Radio/TV Services, and I wasted no time in asking him if he had any interest in working with me in our office as a student worker dealing with Radio/TV. There was never a doubt in my mind that he would be a perfect fit with not only his experience in the field, but maybe more importantly, his commitment and love for the university. It's something I had witnessed repeatedly during my association with him in the news field in prior years. I hired Todd as a student assistant in Radio/TV services, and he immediately proved my original feelings accurate. The years he was an undergraduate at the university were years from which we all benefited. He brought a vibrancy and enthusiasm matched by very few and quickly became a familiar face across campus. While Todd always did his usual outstanding job and completed assignments, it was during this time that it was easy to see that he gave so much more than just what was expected.

One point illustrates that. Western athletics has always been an important part of the university's image. When it was determined by the athletics area that there needed to be some more excitement pumped into basketball games, Todd was there to provide not only his input, but also his own personal sound system equipment. He used it at the basketball games for pre-game, intermission, and halftime music to get the crowd excited. He truly was a part of the initial marketing efforts for fans at Hilltopper basketball games. He committed his own personal time and resources as part of enhancing the fans' experience for games. It was just another extra mile that Todd was always looking for and willing to go.

How he managed to work all of this in along with his basketball officiating and other numerous Scottsville civic and personal activities is still a mystery to me, but he was always there when called upon.

Helping at Western games wasn't the only place he played an important role. I spent a number of years working with Todd at the Lady Invitational of the South high school girls' basketball tournament each December. He worked diligently as the director of the event, which brought not only Kentucky's best girl's high school basketball teams to Scottsville, but some of the nation's best as teams from Oregon, Tennessee, Mississippi, and other states traditionally made a visit to the annual tournament. To top it off, he even arranged to have a team from Australia play one year. I will never forget that year, as the cultural differences the Aussie players brought to Scottsville were eye opening to say the least. [i.e. changing into uniforms in the middle of the high school's hallway at times] Years later, when I visited Australia for a couple of weeks, it certainly brought back images and memories of Todd and his never say never attitude when it came to accomplishments both personally and professionally.

When it came time for Todd to graduate from Western [actually about a semester before], there was never any doubt we had to find a way and place to keep him at the university. It was an easy decision to create an intern/graduate assistant position in the office to keep Todd and his professional expertise around as long as possible. Within a year after he began working in the Radio/TV position, I had the opportunity to change my career path a little at the university by moving into the Special Events area of our department.

While preparing for the move, the question of filling the Radio/TV position didn't take long to answer. There was no doubt that the best person for the position was right in front of us. Yes, there would be the official hiring process to go through, but there was little doubt that after the process, Todd would come through as the best candidate for the job; the process began, but little did anyone know that the best-laid plans could change without notice.

In the summer of 1995, Todd entered the UK Medical Center Hospital with some challenges he seemed to face annually with his cystic fibrosis disease. As long as I had known Todd, there was always the health challenge he had at times with this disease; however, Todd had always beaten any odds with it and in my mind, this was just another minor bump that he would overcome. In Todd, I had witnessed an individual who would never admit defeat in any capacity. Not only would he not admit it, he proved repeatedly through his attitude [and maybe a little stubborn-ness], his will over any obstacle that appeared in front of him.

Since I had met Todd, I had seen him battle the CF disease time and time again and come out the winner in it all. Through all of this, I came to know a man who inspired everyone he met. He especially inspired me with his will, zest, and outlook to always not only overcome odds, but also make a lasting impres-sion on how he went about overcoming them.

It was probably only appropriate that I learned of the news that Todd's final battle with CF was one that would coincide with an annual highlight at WKU, homecoming. Homecoming is a special time at Western. It is a time to reflect and appreciate all that the university on "The Hill" has been to its graduates and family. It's a time to appreciate the special memories and friend-ships made through the lives that Western has influenced.

That homecoming ended up being one to especially reflect about an individual who represented throughout his life what Western is all about: "The Spirit Makes the Master." If there is anyone who epitomized that creed, it was Todd Gibbs. I can think of no one I have met through my personal and professional career at WKU that continues to have an impact on what I strive to make a personal outlook on life. Each and every homecoming since has been a time to remember Todd and all he meant to me personally and professionally.

While not always successful, I know that the efforts I do make to live life every day to its fullest are a direct reflection and tribute to the impression that Todd Gibbs left with not only me, but also everyone he met and impacted. For that, he will forever be a role model in my life.

TODD'S JOURNEY

THROUGH THE EYES OF A
COMMUNITY LEADER

DR. DERO DOWNING,
PRESIDENT EMERITUS, WESTERN
KENTUCKY UNIVERSITY

Rarely have I seen or known of persons who are remembered with the respect, admiration, and love, which surrounded Todd Gibbs. Todd possessed in abundance the qualities most admired in a man. I only wish that we were moved and motivated at the time to have kept a journal describing specific events or occasions when in the company of Todd. It would be a voluminous file recording his remarkable achievements, his acts of kindness, his innate concern for the welfare of others, his many talents, his unwavering faith in God, and his indomitable courage.

None of the above characteristics was worn like a badge or pronouncement. They were simply a part of the person he was, forever positive, strongly committed to excellence in every endeavor, and a determination to make a difference. The fact that Todd experienced serious health problems from an early age did not deter him from reaching for the stars. In fact, he often gave encouragement and assistance to others when he might well have sought greater comfort and relief from his own hurting.

Passing years have made it more difficult than I would like to admit in remembering the conditions, reasons, and circumstances associated with my personal encounters with Todd, each of which was a joy and never failing to inspire. However, dimmed recollections do not in any way lessen the happiness and joy of being in the company of one so brave, compassionate, and determined.

I had engaged in conversations with friends and kinfolk in Allen County in which they shared with noticeable pride the influence for good of one of their favorite sons in Scottsville, Todd Gibbs. They expressed amazement for his young life so well lived in Christ and in his courageous battle with cystic fibrosis. They were well aware of and greatly impressed by the leadership that Todd provided through his role as a city councilman, news reporter, radio commentator, and masterful communicator.

A highly regarded educator who served in positions of importance including the Superintendent of Schools in Allen County-Scottsville was a former student and long time friend of mine, Jimmy Bazzell. There had been occasions when Jimmy described in my presence the widespread pride in and affection for a student who had captivated the hearts and minds of his teachers, fellow students, and all who knew him, Todd Gibbs.

With this background, and considering the repeated expressions of admiration for Todd, my first actual encounter was not a surprise. It was in late spring or early summer of 1990 when I received a phone call from Todd stating that he was representing the planning committee in preparation for a Jimmy Bazzell retirement program to honor Jimmy and to recognize his years of dedicated service to the Allen County Scottsville Schools. Todd had done his homework as evidenced in our discussion about my personal and professional regard for Jimmy, my association with him as an educational colleague and our long-standing friendship. I assured Todd that I would feel genuinely honored to attend and speak at the program.

The ensuing days reaffirmed the traits that Todd possessed and that were legendary in conversations with those who knew, respected, and appreciated him. A masterful communicator and carefully attentive to every detail, Todd kept me informed on the progress of their preparations for the occasion. Nothing was omitted, as he was decisive, remarkably well organized, and gracious in his communication. My wife, Harriet, and I arrived at the designated site for the retirement program where we were met by a member of the committee and escorted to the auditorium.

Todd greeted us with a warm hug and an exuberant smile. It was immediately apparent that he was the program leader, and that nothing had been left to chance. It was an evening, which we have often recalled with much pleasure, and with resounding appreciation for the talents, knowledge, and poise of the M.C., Todd Gibbs. To say that it was well done is an understatement. So greatly impressed by the leadership role that Todd graciously, effectively, and impressively fulfilled, Harriet and I remained after the program for the expressed purpose of commending him and to fellowship with his mother, LaRecea, with whom Harriet had the pleasure of being seated during the program.

Todd revealed the fact that he had enrolled in a class at Western [Journalism] during the fall semester of '89, and was a full-time student in the term just ended, resulting in credit for eighteen semester hours with a B average. Recognizing that Todd represented the meaning of one of Western's most cherished ideals, Life More Life, I urged him and his mother to give Western the opportunity to support his efforts to continue his education. We agreed that if his health permitted, and if they were receptive, we would meet soon to explore ways to accomplish that goal.

Todd had that unique quality which some define as a self-starter. He soon came to the campus under his own initiative where he enrolled for six semester hours in the summer session. That provided the launching pad for successive semesters of academic excellence culminating in his receipt of the A.B. Degree, graduating in May 1994.

Throughout the months described above, I was favored with periodic visits by Todd when he would take time from a demanding class and work schedule to come to the College Heights Foundation. I served there in a part-time capacity following retirement from the position of President, Western Kentucky University. Never one to seek favors or praise, but always unselfish to the core, more often than not Todd brought with him one or more friends or acquaintances whom he had learned were in need of financial help, or had problems that needed attention. He had the compassion and the capacity to detect or sense when someone was in need of help, and those with such conditions seemed to gravitate to Todd like a giant magnet.

There were times when engaging in conversations with Todd, that there was overwhelming evidence of the depth of his feelings revealing his understanding of, sensitivity to, and experience with the major currents of life. It reflected his uncanny insight, and was meaningful testimony to Todd's devotion to and love for his family. He spoke of the many ways in which he was blessed by a loving mother and sisters, all of whom he obviously worshipped. Never dwelling upon matters associated with his fragile health, Todd made mention of his gratitude for the love and support that came from his loved ones, his mother, LaRecea, and his sisters, Hope and Angela, at times with their own personal disregard and sacrifice.

Other personal qualities so often reserved for those of longer life, experience, and maturity, were deep sense of civic responsibility, loyalty, personal integrity, and service. It is through these and other examples of his sterling character that Todd touched my life, that of his fellow students, and all with whom he associated while attending and working at Western Kentucky University.

Among the most gratifying developments in Todd's years, as a student at Western was the bond of friendship that he cultivated with Dr. Kelly Thompson [*President Emeritus of Western*] also associated at that time with the College Heights Foundation. I recall the first time they met, and one could immediately see that bonding of mutual love and devotion. Knowing of Todd's struggle with cystic fibrosis, Dr. Thompson told him of the ill-

LaRecea Gibbs

ness that eventually took the life of his son, Hardin, at the time he was a student at Western.

Dr. Thompson and Todd had similar interests, and it was a source of pride and elation that they shared their experiences associated with the Office of University Relations at Western. Prior knowledge of the influence for good, which was the history of Todd's life, spurred Dr. Thompson to give added encouragement. Like Todd, he was a master at inspiring others. I recall one such occasion when Dr. Thompson quoted the motto of Western, "The Spirit Makes the Master." Then, intently peering into Todd's eyes, he said. "My son, you exemplify that spirit, and you make it real."

At the risk of allowing these observations to be viewed by some as overly personal, I feel compelled to share the following. Born in 1896, my mother was denied the formal educational opportunities of today's world. However, in the completion of the eight grades available at that time, and with her life devoted to the rearing of seven children, Mom was our inspiration and educational anchor post. She read widely and loved literature, poetry, and her Bible. She was often recalling and reciting a particular poem or an old ballad, which in her mind fit a particular gathering, program, or occasion. Therefore, I resort to that same inclination when thinking of Todd, and recalling his widespread influence.

More than forty years ago, Mom sent to each of her seven children a copy of the poem, "Living Sermon." Let me quote here only an excerpt from that poem.

THE LIVING SERMON

I'd rather see a sermon
Than hear one any day,
I'd rather one would walk with me
Than merely tell the way.
The lectures you deliver
May be very wise and true,
But I'd rather get my lessons
By observing what you do.
I may not understand
The high advice you give,
But there's no misunderstanding
How you act and how you live.

At the bottom of that poem, she penciled in this message, "Let's try harder to live each day that others may see Christ in us."

When thinking of Todd, I have repeatedly recalled this poem and the penned admonition of our mother. From an early age, Todd's life was a *living sermon*. He left no question as to his Christian faith, as it was a testimony to *how he acted and how he lived.*

When Todd set aside his sword and shield succumbing to the complications from cystic fibrosis, he rose to be among God's angels. Though his body is no longer among us, he lives on in spirit and in the hearts and minds of family, friends, and neighbors. A line from a well-known hymn gives reassurance of his immortality. It asserts, "You ask me how I know he lives, he lives within our hearts." Todd lives on through the example he set, the people he inspired, the love he gave, the courage he displayed, and his service to all around him.

Note: A portion of the profits of this book will go to the Kentucky Cystic Fibrosis Services. The organization has been in existence for over twenty-five years and has helped numerous patients and families that receive care at the cystic fibrosis clinic at the University of Kentucky Medical Center. They help needy families with paying for vitamins, medications, equipment, college scholarships, and while the patient is hospitalized, meal tickets, parking and gas cards, etc. KCFS also helps pay for the expenses of their family education day each year. Funds to KCFS come from a variety of sources such as local fund raisers held by families, donations in memory of patients who have died and a car show. Personal donations can be made to: KCFS, PO Box 23512, Lexington, KY 40523. The Tax Free # for KCFS is 61–0945743. Thank you for your generosity.

THE TODD GIBBS MEMORIAL SCHOLARSHIP

After Todd's death, a scholarship was established by his family and friends to honor his memory. It is a four year, full tuition scholarship based upon the way Todd lived his life. We look for someone who, in spite of some type of obstacle, has contributed to their school, community, or church through determination and hard work. Any student who attends or plans to attend Western Kentucky University in Bowling Green, KY is eligible.

For more information, contact andy.wagoner@wku.edu or jeff.younglove@wku.edu or alexander.downing@wku.edu.